George Tyrrell, Adolphe Hatzfeld, E. Holt

Saint Augustine

George Tyrrell, Adolphe Hatzfeld, E. Holt

Saint Augustine

ISBN/EAN: 9783337335700

Printed in Europe, USA, Canada, Australia, Japan

Cover: Foto ©Lupo / pixelio.de

More available books at **www.hansebooks.com**

The Saints

SAINT AUGUSTINE

Authorised Translation

All Rights Reserved

SAINT AUGUSTINE

BY

AD. HATZFELD

TRANSLATED BY
E. HOLT

WITH A PREFACE AND NOTES BY
GEORGE TYRRELL, S.J.

In certis, unitas; in dubiis, libertas; in omnibus, caritas.
S. AUGUSTINE.

LONDON
DUCKWORTH & CO., 3, HENRIETTA STREET, W.C.

NEW YORK, CINCINNATI & CHICAGO:　　　　DUBLIN:
BENZIGER BROS.　　　　　　　　　M. H. GILL & SON.

1898

PREFACE

IT will be seen that in some sense M. Hatzfeld has done little more than make St Augustine speak for himself and produce a rapid impression of his personality on our minds which might have been derived more slowly from a promiscuous perusal of his writings. After a brief sketch of the life of the saint and penitent, pieced together mainly from the "Confessions," he gives us in two short sections a general review of the teaching of the great founder of scientific theology in the West.

Yet slight as this work may seem, it will be of no small value if it makes St Augustine and his teaching known even in rough outline to numbers who have neither the leisure nor the ability to do for themselves what M. Hatzfeld has done for them; still more, if it creates a desire in more thoughtful minds to enter into closer sympathy with a great soul, the contemplation of whose depth and width, as it were of some calm ocean expanse, stills and tranquillises our troubled spirits, and makes them for a moment forget their own littleness.

One cannot but lament the number of those to whom the "Confessions" is practically a sealed book; the fewness of those to whom it is in any sense their daily bread. No doubt when the press made it possible to deluge the world with floods of spiritual literature it was bound to be crowded out and forgotten to a large extent. Without any fear of being thought an obscurantist, and wholly in the interests of true spiritual enlightenment, which depends little on information and much upon thought, little on knowledge, much upon wisdom, one may heartily wish back those days when men had to feed their souls on a few works of inspiration, digested and worked into the memory and understanding and will; and not as now on the latest spiritual novelty of the season which piety stimulated by trade has brought forth; when they discovered a thousand thoughts hidden in a single word, while we now look vainly for a single thought under a thousand words.

It is perhaps this same prolific fancifulness of interpretation in St Augustine that deters the severely unimaginative modern mind from the study of his works,—or rather of his spirit, the real thing worth studying. Here, as in the reading of the Hebrew Scriptures and in kindred cases, we are disposed to take everything *au grand serieux*, to forget the writer's "mood and tense," to fail hopelessly in the endeavour to throw ourselves into his subjective attitude. We take his words at the value they would have, spoken by ourselves here and now, thus ignoring that canon of true criticism enunciated by À Kempis: All scripture should be read with that spirit wherewith it was written (i. 5).

Revolted by what seem to us puerilities of

exegesis, by historical and scientific blunders, we attribute to the writer the defects of the language and apparatus he found ready to hand; and are impatient as though they argued in him then, the mental incapacity they would argue in ourselves now. Thus the pearls of great price buried in the " Ennarationes super Psalmos " and elsewhere, in these days are rarely sought and more rarely found.

Yet it may be that the same liberal spirit which has evoked Dante from the tomb and freed him from his cerements may bring to light many treasures hidden away in the folios of Augustine and unmarked even by the theological explorer as he passes by in search of other gains. Unlike as his difficulties were to ours in some respects, yet the solvent he applied to them is of universal and eternal potency, and the same hand which led him, like another wandering star of our own century, " ex umbris et imaginibus in veritatem," or like Dante himself, from darkness to clear vision, is ever held out for the guiding of like souls by like methods. Whatever varying form its doubts may take the " anima naturaliter Christiana "—the truth-loving soul—preserves its type unchanged in all ages; and though Manicheans, Pelagians and Donatists are no more, yet minds are still perplexed about the existence and origin of evil, about liberty and Divine foreknowledge, about the true conception of ecclesiastical unity; while the truth by whose apprehension St Augustine was delivered from the errors of his day, is the self-same to which those of our own day are opposed. One would not look for a refutation of current problems in his pages, but one comes away from the study stronger to deal with them and filled with the spirit in which alone they can be met,—the comprehensive sympathy of one who has himself not merely formulated but felt (even though he may not have yielded to) every doubt which he would vanquish.

But all his controversy put together has not done so much for the faith as has the book of his "Confessions," perhaps the most exquisitely delicate piece of self-analysis that the world has seen yet, where in no spirit of morbid introspection, nor with any of the intellectual inquisitiveness of Montaigne, nor even with any sensitive intention of apology or self-defence, he looks back and recounts step by step the wanderings of his soul in its passage from death unto life, making his "confession," that is, as the word meant in his usage,[1] his thanksgiving or acknowledgment of all that God has done for him, and this, with as little self-consciousness and with all the simplicity of Mary's Magnificat, and before no public but God and His angels, unless it were with a side glance at "Thy servants, my masters," that they too may help him to praise God and be in turn helped by the record of his errors and experiences.

No intellectual fencings will save our faith if the

---

[1] *E.g.* Looking back on his work, he says: Ecce narravi tibi multa quae potui, et quae volui: quoniam tu prior voluisti ut *confiterer* tibi Domino Deo meo quoniam bonus es; quoniam in saeculum misericordia tua.

soul have lost a certain touch with God, which Augustine seemed to preserve through even his worst periods of moral deviation, a certain "creatureliness" of mind with which the book of the "Confessions" is instinct; a sense of our helplessness in the face of those ultimate problems which are at the same time of the last importance for the conduct of our life; a sense that in these matters we are, and are intended to be, as dependent on God as the babe on its mother. We have been told that Newman's faith was allied to scepticism, and the remark though ill-intended is not ill. The purest and highest faith is that of a mind which has learnt its own littleness, which is perfect in self-knowledge. A point in that process is reached when the impatient and proud man will have nothing because he cannot have all, and ignores the little he *can* know because he cannot know more; while the calmer and humbler mind accepts its limitations and passes easily from doubt to faith, so that in some sort the same disposition favours either issue, as wheat and tares are fostered in the same soil, by the same sunshine and rain. In this way scepticism and faith, despair and hope, are close together in many cases, as death and life may be ere the balance is determined one way or the other.

It is this "creaturely" spirit which breathes in every line of Augustine's "Confessions" that lends them their healing influence, and will foster in the reader a disposition which is far more needful for the preservation of his faith than any system of apologetic.

PREFACE

If then M. Hatzfeld's work awakens in some a curiosity to know more about this great human-hearted penitent, saint, and doctor; this son of Monica's tears, whose interest, like that of all great souls, is not local but universal, not of one century, but of all, it will not have been in vain.

The translator has followed (with occasional alterations) Dr Pusey's version of the "Confessions," which, however obscure and unmusical at times, has at least the merit of fidelity to the letter; whereas M. Hatzfeld's fairly free paraphrases done into English would have been two removes from the Latin. Finally, it has always been thought better in dealing with the author's French, to secure a readable English rendering at the cost of certain venial infidelities to the original than to observe that pedantic precision which is needful and excusable only in the translation of an ancient classic.

G. T.

LONDON, *May 4th*, 1898.

LETTER FROM HIS EMINENCE CARDINAL PERRAUD TO THE AUTHOR

AUTUN, *March* 14*th*, 1 97.

SIR,—On my return, after nearly three weeks absence, I found your "St Augustine" on my desk. I feel I cannot thank you for it without congratulating you on having so successfully summed up the life and works, the philosophical and theological doctrine, of this incomparable doctor and father of the Church.

Reading your book has called up before me tender and touching memories. In the far distant days of my young priesthood, I made a pilgrimage to Ostia with the Abbé Henri Perreyve, with whom I was staying in Rome. We were careful to take with us a volume of "the Confessions," and we read the colloquy on "Eternal Blessedness," which inspired Ary Scheffer, while kneeling in the little church built on the site of the house where Augustine and Monica lived. It will soon be four years since I went to Carthage, where I was summoned to preach the funeral oration of Cardinal Lavigerie.

I have prayed in that little church above the ancient harbour, which they call the Chapel of the Tears of St Monica. A few days afterwards I visited the ruins of Hippo, where I saw part of the walls of the Basilica of Peace, and I had the happiness of hearing Holy Mass at Bône before the very precious relic of the right arm of St Augustine—that right arm which has written so many masterpieces. I am sure you must have experienced a great spiritual joy in writing these pages which will help to make "the son of so many tears" known, admired, and loved.

Believe me to remain, Sir,

Your very respectfully devoted,

† Adolphe Louis Albert,
Card. Perraud,
Bishop of Autun.

INTRODUCTION

ONE finds in the life of St Augustine a model of Christian holiness, slowly and laboriously formed in a soul long darkened by error, and led astray by passion. To no one, indeed, better applies the text chosen by Bossuet for the funeral oration of Anne of Gonsaga: "I have taken thee by the hand to bring thee back from the ends of the earth. I have called thee from far distant places; I have chosen thee, and I have not cast thee away; fear not, for I am with thee."

We cannot gaze unmoved at these internal conflicts, these alternate defeats and victories in a heart which at the same moment is a slave to the world and thirsting for God; and as we gaze we draw from the sight a consoling hope for our own moral miseries. Assuredly there is among the saints no single one whose history does not offer to Christians a keen interest, and a precious lesson; but it always seems that we are touched most closely by the lives of those who have been great sinners before becoming great saints; that we feel most drawn to those who have known and succumbed to human weakness. The example of these brilliant and striking conversions is a powerful encouragement to us in our days of depression, and bids us never to despair of ourselves, since the greatest faults can never exhaust the Divine Mercy. "Let those," says Bossuet, "fear to show the defects of holy souls who know not how powerful is the arm of God to cause the same defects not only to show forth His glory, but even to serve for the perfecting of His elect. As for us, we know how the denials of his Lord by St Peter, the persecutions which St Paul inflicted on the Church, and the errors of St Augustine, have served in the fashioning of the soul of each."

This story also offers a peculiar interest and encouragement to Christian mothers, for in it they may perceive that the tears and the prayers of St Monica, the mother of Augustine, were the instruments which God used to lead him back from such a distance. God willed that the sanctity of the son should be at once the work of the maternal piety, and the reward of her faith.

But St Augustine was not only a holy priest, an indefatigable Apostle, a courageous shepherd always ready to give his life for his flock; he was, so to say, the creator of Western theology, having brought forward, argued, and resolved the most difficult questions with an admirable science and a sureness of perception drawn only from the reading and meditation of the holy books.

Others have enlightened this or that point of doctrine, he alone has thrown light on all equally. "It is a fact that one cannot deny," says Bossuet, "that St Athanasius, for example, who yields nothing in genius or depth to any of the Fathers, and who is, as one may say, the coryphæus of the Church in the arguments against Arius, goes little beyond this matter. It is almost the same with the other Fathers, whose theology appears confined to the subjects which the occasion and the needs of the Church presented to them. It was permitted by God that St Augustine should have all sorts of heresies to combat.

Manicheism gave him the opportunity to treat of the depths of the Divine nature, of creation, Providence, the nothingness from which all things have been drawn, and of the free will of man, in which he must look for the cause of evil; in short, of the authority and perfect conformity of the two Testaments. Donatism caused him to discuss minutely and from their basis the efficacy of the sacraments and the authority of the Church.

Having had to contend with the Arians in Africa, he left this important matter more strongly enforced and more clearly explained than it was before. He spoke of the Incarnation of the Son of God with as much accuracy and profundity as they did afterwards at Ephesus, or rather he preceded the decisions of that council.

The Pelagian sect gave occasion to this learned Father to uphold the foundation of Christian humility, and by explaining thoroughly the spirit of the New Covenant, he developed the principles of Christian morality. So that one may say of St Augustine, that all the dogmas of religion, speculative as well as practical, having been so profoundly explained by him, he is the only one of the Fathers through whom

Providence has designed, by means of the disputes which arose during his times, to give us a body of theology, which is the fruit of his continual and profound study of the sacred books" (Bossuet, *Défense de la Tradition et des Saints Pères*, iv. 16). And this theologian, who is witnessed for by such an authoritative voice, is at the same time a great philosopher, one to whom all historians of philosophy give a place in their works, amongst the metaphysicians who have thrown light on human thought. "For the principles of pure philosophy," says La Bruyère, "for their application and development, for the justness of conclusions, the dignity of language, and the beauty of morality and feeling, one can compare nothing to St Augustine except Plato, and Cicero" (La Bruyère, *Des Esprits forts*). Fénelon goes much further. "I should believe St Augustine much sooner than Descartes on matters of pure philosophy; for besides his having reconciled them so much better with religion, there is also in this Father a much greater exercise of genius in all metaphysical truths, even though he may only have treated them, just as occasion offered, without any particular order. If an enlightened man were to gather from the books of St Augustine all the sublime truths which he has scattered through them, as if by chance, this selection would be far superior to "the meditations" of Descartes, though these meditations are the greatest effort of that philosopher's genius" (Fén., *Lett. sur la Religion*, iv. 16).

Without wishing, however, to compare these two

great minds, it is certain that St Augustine merits the name of philosopher. He not only wishes, with the Catholic Church, that reason should be the support of faith, but he gives to reason all that can be attributed to it without prejudice to faith; or rather he seeks, as St Thomas Aquinas did later, to establish between reason and faith a fruitful alliance. At the same time that he teaches revealed truths, he establishes on rational proofs all the truths to which human reason can attain by its own powers; he introduces them into the statement of Christian dogmas to render these more accessible; and although he has not, like St Thomas, composed a body of philosophical doctrine regularly arranged, one may say that there is no question relating to the human soul, to the world, and to God, on which he has not in passing thrown lights as deep as they are original.

We may add that, although the saints do not belong to any country, and though the entire Church claims them as her children, without distinction of origin, St Augustine, Bishop of Hippo, seems to belong to France, since Hippo was formerly in that part of Africa which now belongs to France, and the town of Bône has been built on the ruins of Hippo, and on a neighbouring hill a monument to St Augustine's honour has been raised by the French bishops. St Augustine was buried at Hippo in the crypt of the Basilica of Peace. When the Vandals destroyed the city which he had rendered famous by his apostleship, his tomb was threatened by the Arian barbarians. The island of Sardinia, lying close to Africa, offered a refuge to those who fled into exile to escape the fury of the enemies of the faith. St Fulgentius and several African bishops sought an asylum there and took with them the relics of St Augustine. The town of Cagliari received this sacred deposit, which was placed in the basilica of Saint Saturninus, and was there the object of the veneration of the faithful. But when the Saracens became masters of Sardinia, the pious Luitprand, King of the Lombards, fearing that the bones of the saint might be profaned by the infidels, bought them for their weight in gold, and laid them solemnly in the crypt of the basilica of St Peter at Pavia. At last when the Church regained possession of that part of Africa under the flag of France, the bishop of Algiers and Hippo, Mgr. Dupuech, obtained part of the relics of St Augustine from the chapter of Pavia, and transported them in the midst of an immense concourse of prelates and pilgrims to the new French and Christian Hippo, to the very places where the crowds pressed to listen to his words long ago, and where everything is still full of his memory. In collecting in this book the principal characteristics of his history and his doctrine, we have tried to make him live again as his contemporaries, who loved and revered him, knew him.

First Book

THE LIFE OF SAINT AUGUSTINE

TO relate the story of Saint Augustine's life is to follow him through those mysterious ways by which, after having alienated himself from God, and being conquered, as one might believe, by error and evil, he became one of the lights of the Church, and one of the models of Christian life. The province of Africa which was his birth-place was full of churches and bishoprics. Nowhere had the Christian mission made more proselytes. But paganism reigned there still in manners and customs, and Christian society itself was profoundly divided by heresies which perverted the faith of the people, and fought furiously against one another. The disputes on dogma, or even on points of discipline, were nowhere so fierce as in Africa. The principal sect was that of the Donatists, a kind of cruel rigorists and mystics, offering more than one point of resemblance to the Anabaptists and Independents. Other sects, strangers to Christianity, and purely Oriental, still agitated the turbulent imagination of the inhabitants of Africa. There was no country where the sect of the Manicheans, which had come from the borders of Persia, and had spread itself nearly everywhere over the field of Christianity, had more partisans or more able missionaries. It adopted in part the dogmas of Christian worship, and counterfeited its hierarchy; and it was not rare to find in one little town of a province of Africa, a Catholic bishop, a Donatist bishop, and a Manichean bishop, each with his votaries, contesting the faith of the people, and distributing books and catechisms (Villemain, *Éloquence chrétienne au onzième siècle: St Augustine*). In this restless and corrupt world in which the young Augustine found himself launched, his first impression came to him from the tenderness of a pious mother. Thagaste, a small market-town of Numidia, where he first saw the light, had abandoned the sect of Donatus to return to the Catholic Communion. There Augustine was born, November 13th, 354. His father Patricius was a pagan, a man of a violent character, which had been softened gradually by the patience and humility of Monica his wife. She obtained his consent that Augustine, who was destined for Christianity, should be made a catechumen from his birth without being baptised. At that time they deferred baptism to a later age, but as the assurance of being washed from all faults by the baptismal waters produced grave abuses—some parents not even fearing to say of their sons: "Let them do as they will, they are not yet baptised"—the Church was obliged to proscribe this custom. They made the sign of the Cross on the child's forehead, and they put the blessed salt into his mouth. "I was marked with the sign of the Cross of our Lord, and embalmed with His salt as soon as I issued from the womb of my mother, who had fixed all her hope in Him." Monica nursed him herself and made him imbibe the love of Jesus Christ together with her milk. "This name of my Saviour, Thy Son, I drew it in with my mother's milk, and kept it at the bottom of my heart." She awaked this young soul to the hopes of the Christian faith. "She taught me from my infancy the eternal life which the humility of Thy Son, abased to our pride, has promised to us, O Lord, our God."

The lessons of this tenderly loved mother left a profound mark on Augustine's soul. The incredulity of Patricius could not prevail over the gentle piety of Monica, speaking ever to her child of "his Father who was in Heaven." "She succeeded, O my God, in making Thee more my father than he was" (*Confess.*, i. 11).

Augustine was now growing up, and his precocious intelligence awoke his father's ambition. Patricius dreamt of honours, reputation, and riches for him; he was ready to impose heavy sacrifices on himself, to give a brilliant education to his son.

Augustine went at first to the school at Thagaste. Then, when he had learnt the first elements of letters, his father sent him to the neighbouring town of Madaura, to study grammar, poetry, and rhetoric. There he was noticed for his quick mind and retentive memory. He was inquisitive about everything that appealed to his imagination, eager for emotions, passionately attracted by fictions, and rebellious against all which demanded effort from him. The Greek tongue especially repelled him; but he delighted in the Latin poets, and afterwards he reproached himself with having shed tears over Dido's death, while he remained insensible to the misfortune of having lost God. He accused himself of employing the faculties which he ought to have consecrated to the praise and service of God in seeking for the vain praises of men. He deplored the blindness of those who are more careful to speak well than to act well, and who fear more to commit a solecism in their discourse than to sin against their Lord.

While his father, careful only for his earthly future and his fortune, put him through the apprenticeship of profane letters, his mother, with her eyes fixed on another future, led him to the school of Jesus Christ; and the child prayed on his knees to the Saviour to keep him from punishment when he had committed some fault.

"When I was still a child I implored Thee to be my support and my refuge, my tongue was loosened to invoke Thee; and as a little one I begged of Thee with the greatest fervour not to let me be beaten at school" (*Confess.*, i. 9).

His faults were frequent, and sometimes grave; it is from himself that we learn it in his admirable "Confessions"—that sincere history of a soul which has made, not an exhibition, but an humble avowal of its errors, a severe examination of its conscience before God and men, as at the time of public confession; and which, ashamed and repentant, is never weary of blessing the infinite mercy which has raised it from such a depth.

He condemned his childhood very severely as biassed towards evil.

"I say and I confess before Thee, my God, how I thought that to obtain the admiration of those who praised me was to live well. I did not see the gulf of corruption into which I was plunging far from Thy gaze.

"For what could there be more guilty than I in my actions, when, forgetting whom I was displeasing, I deceived by continual lies my governor, my masters, my parents, enticed by my love of gambling, or by my taste for vain shows and the wish to imitate them? I also stole provisions from the cellar, or the table of my parents, either for greediness or to give other children, who made me pay them for playing with me, though it was a pleasure to them. In these same games I often got the victory by cheating, yielding to the vain pride of victory over the others; and there was nothing with which I was more impatient and which I reproached more angrily in the others, if I chanced to discover it, than just what I was doing to them. But if I was caught myself, I flew into a violent rage sooner than own it.

"Is this, then, the innocence of children? No, Lord, it does not exist. I take you to witness, my God! It begins with tutors and masters, with nuts and balls, and birds, to pass afterwards to magistrates and kings, to gold, to lands, and to slaves, the object of passion changing according as they advance in age, so that the ferule is replaced later by graver chastisements" (*Confess.*, i. 18).

The innate corruption of the sons of Adam weighs

on the child* as on the man before he is washed in the waters of baptism; he is born a sinner; it is the original stain. "If I have been conceived in iniquity, and my mother has nourished me in sin within her womb, where then, I demand, my God, where and when, my Lord, have I Thy slave been innocent?" (*Confess.*, i. 7).

However, he recognised that there was also good alongside of the evil. In the midst of the faults which Augustine confesses, the germs of those rare qualities show themselves which should one day make a great saint and a great bishop. He imputes the evil to himself, the good he credits to God. "I kept by an interior instinct the integrity of my reason. In my little thoughts about little things, I loved truth, and I did not wish to be deceived. I was well gifted with memory; and friendship delighted me. I fled from meanness and ignorance, as well as from suffering. How many things worthy of admiration and praise show themselves in this little being! And all these are the gifts of my God. I have not given them to myself. These are treasures, and these treasures are myself. He who has made me is good, and He is Himself my Treasure. And it is to Him that I render thanks with rapture, for all the treasures I possessed as a child" (*Confess.*, i. 18).

As he was emerging from childhood, he fell seriously ill, and they feared for his life. He immediately begged of his mother to have him baptised; but the illness yielding to treatment,

* See Appendix.

Monica thought it wiser to defer baptism. Augustine regretted his mother's determination later on, saying to himself that perhaps the virtue of the sacrament might have preserved him; Monica's fear was, on the contrary, that the sacrament might be profaned by the impulses of youth.

"Thou hast seen, Lord, when I was still a child, that I was attacked suddenly by colic, and a fever which threatened my life. And with what faith and eagerness of soul I besought from the piety of my mother, and from Thy Church, the common mother of us all, the baptism of Thy Christ, my God and my Lord. And how the mother of my flesh, whose chaste heart full of trouble desired above all to bring forth my eternal salvation in Thy faith, was hastening to prepare everything that I might be initiated, and washed in this salutary sacrament, and that I might confess Thee, Lord Jesus, for the remission of my sins, when I was suddenly cured. My baptism was then put off as if it had been as inevitable that I should sin still, as that I should live; and because sins committed after baptism were considered much graver and more dangerous. . . . It might have been better that I had recovered later, that by the zeal of me and mine I might have received health of soul, and that it might have been preserved to me by Thy protection who had given it to me! But what waves of temptation were going to break over me! My mother foresaw them, and she preferred to deliver over to them the clay from which one day a new man should be born, than his image already formed" (*Confess.*, i. 11).

Augustine resumed his lessons at school successfully, but it was not long before he left Madaura for higher instruction. His father wished him to finish his studies in the renowned schools of Carthage; but as the resources of Patricius were not sufficient, it took almost a year to procure the necessary money. This delay was fatal to Augustine. During the year he spent with his family he gave himself up entirely to pleasure.

"There was no one who did not praise my father for giving me, even beyond what he could afford, the means of pursuing my studies abroad, for even fathers much richer than he was did not do as much for their children. But this father never troubled himself to know how I was growing up, or if I was chaste, provided I was cultured, however wanting in the culture which comes from Thee, my God, and Thee alone, the kind and true Master of this heart, Thy domain" (*Confess.*, ii. 3.). Freed from the tutelage of his masters, idle, and given up to himself, Augustine began to yield to the temptations by which he was surrounded; he abandoned himself to pleasure, and carried into it all the fire of his passionate nature.

"I thirsted to satiate myself with gross pleasures, from the time of my adolescence; I did not fear to grow wild again in secret and shadowy amours; my beauty faded, and in Thine eyes, Lord, I was nothing more than corruption, humouring myself, and seeking only to please men. From the miry depths of the concupiscence of the flesh, rose thick vapours, the ferments of puberty, which, veiling and obscuring my soul, no longer allowed me to discern pure love through these mists of passion. And their confused bubbling up drew my feeble youth towards the gulf of iniquity. Thine anger weighed heavy on me and I perceived it not" (*Confess.*, ii. 1, 2).

But a soul such as his could not find repose in this life of disorder. "Thou wert always there, Lord, striking me in Thy mercy, spreading the most cruel bitterness over my guilty joys, to teach me that there is no happiness for him who offends Thee." His mother tried in vain to arrest him on this fatal descent. "I listened to her counsels as to a woman's talk, which I should be ashamed to obey. And yet these counsels came from Thee, my God, and I did not know it. I believed that Thou wert silent, and that it was she who spake when Thou spakest by her mouth; it was Thee I despised in her, I, her son; I, the son of Thy handmaid; I Thy servant" *Confess.*, ii. 3).

All this time Monica wept and prayed unceasingly, putting her trust in God alone.

However, Romanianus, one of the principal inhabitants of Thagaste, whose liberality had caused him to be elected "Protector" of the city, interesting himself in the progress of Augustine, supplied from his purse the money which Patricius needed, and, thanks to his generosity, Augustine was able to set out for Carthage towards the end of the year 370, being then seventeen. The following year, he lost his father, whom Monica had in the end succeeded in converting to the Christian faith.

No place could have been more dangerous for him than this great town.

If Carthage was a centre of learning, where the most able masters of letters and science were assembled together, it was also, and above all, a centre of pleasure, where paganism, still deep-rooted, exhibited its licentious spectacles, where the worship of Astarte displayed its impure feasts; where the ordinary seductions of great towns flowed in, where manners were relaxed, and where elegant vice seemed to the young men a mark of glory. Greedy at once of this equivocal glory as well as of literary fame, Augustine led openly and with equal fervour the life of study and the life of pleasure. He attended the schools, devoted himself to Virgil, and shone especially in the practice of rhetoric, but, surrounded by his debauched companions, he never resisted temptation. "When one heard the others say: 'Come, let us do this or that,' one would have been ashamed not to have lost all shame" (*Confess.*, ii. 9).

Afterwards, he blushed for this emulation in evil, but then, it flattered his vanity. "I was walking towards the precipice so blindly, that in the midst of companions of my own age I was ashamed of being less vicious than they, when I heard them boasting of their vile acts, and pluming themselves upon them, in proportion as they were disgraceful. And I delighted in doing evil, not only from thirst of enjoyment, but from thirst of glory. . . .

"What is to be despised if not vice? And I, for fear of being despised, made myself out more vicious than I was; and when I had not committed enough excesses to equal the most depraved, I boasted of those which I had not done, fearing that the more I had restrained myself, the more despicable I should appear " (*Confess.*, ii. 3).

A more stable attachment came to temper, without correcting, this dissolute life.

"At this time I was living with a woman, who was not united to me by the legitimate tie of marriage, and whom I had only sought to satisfy a vague and thoughtless desire. At the same time, I saw no one but her, and I lived faithfully with her. But by my own example I already recognised what a distance separates the conjugal union, whose purpose is to bring children into the world, from the illicit union whose fruits appear in spite of us, though when they come we are forced to love them" (*Confess.* iv. 2). In truth, a son was born of this illegitimate connection, Adeodatus, "the son of his sin," as he called him, whom he loved tenderly, and from whom he never separated himself. Although he had not the strength to tear himself from this existence, he continued through the grace of God to feel the emptiness of it, and he did not taste without trouble these enjoyments which he had too eagerly sought. "I fell into this snare of love in which, O! my God, I had so much desired to be taken! By Thy mercy, what gall was spread over the sweetness! From the time that I was loved, and that I could enjoy secretly what had captivated me, I enmeshed myself with a light heart in a network of troubles, where I was struck with the iron rods of jealousy, suspicions, fears, rages, and quarrels" (*Confess*, iii. 1).

The first serious awakening of conscience came to him from pagan philosophy. Ensnared by eloquence, to which he attached all his dreams for the future, Augustine thought only of perfecting this oratorical talent, so much admired by his masters and his fellow-scholars. More skilled in Roman literature than in Greek, which language was less familiar to him, he read and re-read Cicero, whom he had taken for a model. Chance brought under his eyes a work, of which fragments only remain to us; this was "Hortensius," a philosophical dialogue in which Cicero seeks from the study of wisdom the consolation of the painful trials which saddened the close of his life. He brings out this idea; that the study of wisdom never deceives. If all is ended for us at death, is it not a happiness to have passed our life in such noble studies? If our life continues after death, is not the constant search after truth the most assured means of preparing us for this other existence? And will not the soul, who in this meditation has learnt to detach herself from earth, rise more rapidly to the heavenly habitations? Then Cicero enumerates all those who in his time, or before him, had conveyed this wisdom into their lives, and on reading this, Augustine understood how small were the passing interests which formed the subject of eloquence beside the eternal interests which are the object of philosophy.

"There is a book of Cicero's entitled 'Hortensius' which contains an exhortation to philosophy. This book, O my God, changed my sentiments, changed the prayers that I addressed to Thee, and gave me other wishes and desires. I no longer had anything but scorn for foolish hopes, I desired with an incredible ardour the immortality of wisdom, and I began to raise myself to return to Thee" (*Confess.*, iii. 4).

"I longed, my God, to fly from the things of earth to Thee, and I knew not that it was Thou who wast working in me. For in Thee is wisdom, and it was the love of wisdom, or, as the Greeks call it, philosophy, which this book caused to spring in my soul. And what charmed me in these exhortations was, that I felt myself animated and excited by exhortation, to love, to seek, to pursue, to embrace closely, not such or such a sect, but wisdom itself, whatever it might be" (*Confess.*, iii. 4).

At the same time, this purely human wisdom, exalted though it was, was not that which his mother had taught him, and of which the memories of his childhood spoke to him. "One thing cooled my ardour, it was that the name of Christ was not there, and this name, by Thy mercy, Lord, this name of Thy Son, my Saviour, my heart had drawn in with my mother's milk, and kept in its depths; and every doctrine where this name did not appear, fluent, elegant, and truth-like though it might be, could not master me altogether" (*Confess.*, iii. 4).

This thought brought him back to the Sacred Writings, but he could not relish them. The bold simplicity of the Bible repulsed the admirer of classic eloquence, accustomed to the nobility and elegance of Cicero. "I resolved to turn my mind to the Holy Scriptures to see what they were. And here I found those things which are not for the proud to behold, nor even for the humble, without a veil; things mean at the first approach, and afterwards sublime, but veiled in mystery. I was not yet capable of entering in and bowing my head that I might penetrate thither; nor was it with this feeling that I approached the Holy Scriptures: they seemed to me unworthy to be brought into comparison with the majesty of Cicero. My pride, I repeat it, despised the manner in which the things are said, and my intelligence could not discover the hidden sense! They become great only for the humble, but I disdained to humble myself, and, inflated with vain glory, I believed myself great" (*Confess.*, iii. 5).

The same pride made it painful to him to submit, painful to humble this reason, this intelligence of which he was so proud. It was that which flung him into the heresy of the Manicheans, who reproached Catholicism precisely for demanding faith, and declared themselves the true interpreters of the gospel. He tells us this in a treatise, dedicated to his friend Honoratus. "You know, my dear Honoratus, that what made me fall into the snares of the Manicheans, was their assertion that, without using the imperious path of authority, they would lead to God and free from error those who should follow their teaching. In truth, what decided me to follow them, and to listen to them assiduously for nearly nine years, rejecting the holy religion which had been taught me in my childhood, was, that they guaranteed that whereas this same religion imposed the yoke of a superstitious belief on us, and obliged us to believe things without understanding them, they asked no one to believe anything without having first penetrated the truth in such a way as to make it evident. How should I not have been attracted by such promises, in the state of mind in which I found myself when I fell into their hands, full of the presumption of youth; loving the truth, no doubt, but inflated with this pride which one usually contracts in the schools, when one hears men, who are accounted able, descant on all subjects; I myself caring only to argue and to discuss, treating as songs and fables all that was not according to my ideas, at the same time that I had an ardent desire to possess this truth which they promised to make me see clearly" (*De utilit. cred.* i.).

We may add that even the errors of the Manicheans attracted him and allured him from another point of view. Augustine had not yet arrived at conceiving a spiritual nature, which does not fall under the empire of the senses, and is accessible only to pure reason. "I was already beyond my first youth, which I had stained with so many crimes and abominations; I was entering a riper age where it was still more shameful for me to remain wandering after vain imaginations, not being able to conceive of any substance which did not strike the vision. At the same time, I was far from believing, my God, that Thou hadst a body like to a human body. In the case of my soul I had firm confidence that Thy nature is incorruptible, unalterable, and for ever immutable; for though the reasons were unknown to me, I saw clearly and with entire certainty that what can neither change or alter or be corrupted is more perfect and more excellent than what is susceptible of change, alteration, and corruption. Armed with this single truth my heart raised itself against the vain phantoms which beset it, and struggled to scatter the gross and deceptive images which fluttered around it. But the swarm was barely dispersed before it gathered again and obscured my mind, constraining me to conceive of Thee, if not under the form of a human body, at least as of something corporeal, which filled space, and which filled all parts of the universe and extended even infinitely beyond that. . . .

"And I judged of it thus because I could not imagine, except as a pure nothing, all that had not this sort of size and extent which things have that fill a certain space. . . .

"Such was my mind, so weighed down, so blinded by the flesh that I was myself unknown to myself; all that was not capable of extending itself, of spreading itself, or of confining itself in a certain place . . . was for me, as I have said, a pure negation. . . .

"And I took no heed that this action of my mind, by which in some sort I created a corporeal image, was of a different nature from that of the body, and that it could not thus form images to itself, if it had not been in itself something superior" (*Confess.*, vii. 1).

"Thus in my ignorance I always imagined God as

a corporeal substance, not being able to conceive that the soul was any other thing than a body, very subtle doubtless, but contained in a certain habitation, and bounded by a certain space" (*Confess.*, v. 10).

Now the Manicheans admitted of no other substance than matter. For them the principle of good, as the principle of evil, was an extended substance which only differed from the rest of matter in that it was more subtle and more free. It was this corporeal being whom they pretended to adore under the name of God. And the error which darkened the spirit of Augustine was akin to the error of Manicheism.

The existence of the eternal principle of evil seduced him in another way. Impelled by fiery passions, but troubled by the importunate reproaches of his conscience, he wished to excuse himself in his own eyes, and to persuade himself that he was submitting in spite of himself to the tyranny of his inclinations and the irresistible influence of his nature. But at the same time it was repugnant to him to admit that God was the author of evil.

The doctrine of Manes seemed to reconcile everything. It recognised two gods existing together from all eternity; one, the principle of good, inhabiting the abode of light; the other, the principle of evil, inhabiting the place of darkness. The world had been created by the principle of good, but the principle of evil had introduced disorder into this work: and henceforth all creatures bore in them the double mark of these two hostile divinities.

Accordingly there were two souls in man, opposed to each other, as were their authors; the rational soul emanating from the principle of good; and the animal soul emanating from the principle of evil. It was in vain that Manes, in order to accredit his doctrine as Christian, declared that the rational soul could be delivered by the gospel from the empire of the animal soul; he was obliged to admit that man submits in a certain degree to the constraint of the bad spirit; and that the responsibility of sin falls in part on the eternal principle of evil. "I persuaded myself that it is not we who sin, but that it is I know not what foreign nature which sins in us; it satisfied my pride to believe that I was not guilty; and when I had done something wrong, instead of accusing myself, to obtain healing from Thee because I had sinned against Thee, I preferred to excuse myself, and to accuse I know not what other being that was in me, and was not me" (*Confess.*, v. 10).

"Some indefinable sentiment of piety prevented me from believing that God who is good could have created no evil nature; I fixed two substances opposed to each other, both infinite, but the bad more restricted, the good more free. And from this poisonous belief my other sacrileges flowed" (*Confess.*, v. 10).

Monica was overwhelmed at this apostasy of Augustine, and sacrificing her affection to her faith and her duty, she banished her son from her presence, and would not permit him to sit at her table, though he might dwell under her roof. But when he had obeyed, she fell on her knees and wept over this faithless son more bitterly than a mother weeps at the burial of her child.

Yet Augustine was far from being convinced of the error which he professed. Customs, prejudices, ignorance of the truth alone separated him from the true Church. He already felt many doubts as to the teaching of the Manicheans.

Outwardly he remained bound to them but he did not give his heart to the masters who had seduced him. He admired their eloquence but he even began to suspect their capability. Above all he mistrusted a religion which had not sufficient ascendency over him to conquer him completely and render him capable of renouncing and vanquishing his passions.

"That which hindered me from giving myself up entirely to them," he said to Honoratus, in the treatise referred to above, "that which made me confine myself to those whom they called *auditors*, without abandoning the interests and hopes that I might have in the world, was, that I perceived they were far richer in specious arguments for attacking the doctrine of the Church, than in proofs for establishing their own. I had taken them for able men, because they found a great abundance of developments on this subject, and because they had the art of saying ever the same things in a great variety of ways. I had then a bias for this form of talent, and I only understood later that there is nothing in it which is not within the range of every man who is a little learned. As to their principles, they had the skill only to show a few of them, and without approving them altogether, I thought that I could hold them, and content myself with them, not knowing any others which appeared to me more satisfying.

"But you must not think that the least ray of light enlightened me at this time when I breathed only the love of the world, when I was possessed with the criminal hope of feasting my eyes on the frail beauty of a woman, passionately fond of luxury, of the exhibition of riches, and the false renown of honours, and in short given up to all the most culpable delights. For you must surely have remarked that it was these things alone I aspired after during the time that I listened to the Manicheans with more assiduity than pleasure" (*De utilit.*, i.).

From a pupil, Augustine had become a master. He had left Carthage to return to his native town, where he taught grammar and rhetoric. Around him were grouped the young auditors, his faithful disciples, Honoratus, Alypius, Licentius, etc., and the young master, eager for the union of souls, wished to convert his friends to Manicheism, even though he had doubts of it himself. One of them who was particularly dear to him, fell dangerously ill; and while he was unconscious they baptised him. Contrary to all expectation he recovered, and Augustine wished to persuade him not to take this baptism which was administered without his knowledge into consideration; but his friend repulsed him gently, and a short time after he had a relapse and died (*Confess.*, iv. 4.), leaving his friend an example which could not fail to strike him. Augustine was inconsolable for a long time. "At this grief my heart was utterly darkened; and whatever I beheld was death. My native country was a torment to me and my father's house a strange unhappiness; and whatever I had shared with him, without him, became a distracting torture. Mine eyes sought him everywhere but he was not granted to them; and I hated all places for that they had him not; nor could they now tell me: 'He is coming,' as when he was alive and had been absent. I became a great riddle to myself, and I asked my soul, *why she was so sad, and why she disquieted me sorely :*[1] but she knew not what to answer me. And if I said *Trust in God*, she obeyed me not; because that most dear friend, whom she had lost was, being man, both truer and better than that phantasm she was bid to trust in. Tears only were sweet to me, for they succeeded my friend, in the dearest of my affections" (*Confess.*, iv. 4). "For I carried a shattered and bleeding soul, impatient of being borne by me, yet where to repose it I found not. Not in calm groves, not in games and music, nor in fragrant spots, nor in curious banquetings, nor in the pleasures of the bed and the couch; nor (finally) in books or poesy found it repose. All things looked ghastly, yea, the very light; whatsoever was not what he was, was revolting and hateful, except groaning and tears. For in those alone found I a little refreshment" (*Confess.*, iv. 7). The grief of this loss, but also doubtless the ambition to make himself known and to shine

[1] Ps. xlii. 5.

on a larger stage, decided Augustine to leave the town of Thagaste and to establish himself at Carthage. Romanianus, after having tried in vain to keep him in his native town, furnished the money necessary for his journey and his installation.

Augustine never forgot what he owed this generous patron; he expresses his profound gratitude to him in the Dialogue, *Contra Academicos*. "From my youth, you helped me in my need. In the place where I was going to begin my studies, you opened to me your house, your purse, and what is far more, your heart. At the death of my father your friendship consoled me, your words encouraged me, and your liberality came to my assistance. Even in our town you gave me so much of your patronage and friendship that our fellow-citizens respected me almost as much as they did you. When I went to Carthage to exercise higher functions, I confided my project and my hopes to you alone. The love you bore your own town, where I was already teaching, made you hesitate to give your assent, but seeing that you could not conquer the inclination of a young man, aspiring after what tempted his ambition, you, like an admirable friend, came to my help, and furnished me with all that was necessary for my journey. In the same place where you had already nurtured me at the beginning of my studies, you still sustained me when I wished to try my strength, and take to my wings" (*Contr. Academ.*, ii. 2).

Augustine opened a school of eloquence at Carthage, and obtained very brilliant success in it. Round him were grouped Licentius, the son of Romanianus, Eulogius, Honoratus, Nebridius, Alypius of Thagaste, who was to succeed in his heart the friend that he had lost. He mingled moral teaching with the teaching of rhetoric, and we know that one of his lessons in which he censured sharply the games of the Circus, determined Alypius to renounce them.

"The whirlpool of the corruptions of Carthage, where such frivolous spectacles abounded, had engulfed Alypius in a passion for the Circus games, into which he threw himself with deplorable unreserve. But while he was miserably tossed therein, ... as I one day sat in my accustomed place, he entered, greeted me, sat down, and applied his mind to what I then was engaged on. I had by chance a passage in hand, which, while I was explaining, a likeness from the Circensian races occurred to me, as likely to make what I would convey pleasanter and plainer, seasoned with biting mockery of those whom that madness had enthralled. God, Thou knowest that I then thought not of curing Alypius of that infection. But he took it wholly to himself, and thought that I said it simply for his sake. For upon that speech he burst out of that pit so deep, wherein he was wilfully plunged, being blinded with its wretched pleasures, and he shook his mind free with a strong self-command; bade adieu to the lewd spectacles of the Circus, nor came he again thither" (*Confess.*, vi. 7.)

However, Augustine still frequented the Manicheans. And not content with leading his friends to share his error, there was a moment when he dreamt of converting his mother, and he tried to persuade her. But Monica's faith was immoveable. Her prayers had obtained baptism for her husband before his death, and every day she besought the same grace for her son with tears.

At this time she had a dream that Augustine relates to us. " For she saw herself standing on a certain wooden rule,[1] and a shining youth coming towards her, cheerful, and smiling upon her, herself grieving and overwhelmed with grief. But he (not to be instructed, but in order to instruct, as is their wont) enquired of her the causes of her grief and daily tears, and she answering that she was bewailing my perdition, he bade her rest contented, and told her to look and observe, 'That where she was, there was I also'; and when she looked she saw me standing by her on the same rule. . . . When she had told me this vision, and I would fain bend it to mean 'That she rather should not despair of being one day what I was,' she presently without any hesitation replies, 'No, for it was not told me that " where he is, there shalt thou be also; but, Where thou art, there shall he be also!"' . . . And this reply made more impression on me than the dream itself " (*Confess.*, iii. 11.)

"Thou gavest her then another answer by a priest of thine, a certain bishop brought up in Thy

---

[1] See, for the explanation of this rule, the passage given farther on, where Augustine after his conversion thanks God for having firmly established him in that *rule of faith* where He had shewed him unto his mother in a vision so many years before. (*Confess.*, viii. 12.)

Church, and well studied in Thy books. Whom, when this woman had entreated to vouchsafe to converse with me, refute my errors, unteach me ill things, and teach me good things, he refused wisely, as I afterwards perceived. For he answered, that I was yet unteachable, being puffed up with the novelty of that heresy, and had already perplexed divers unskilful persons with captious questions, as she had told him. 'But let him alone a while' (saith he), 'only pray God for him; he will of himself by reading find what that error is, and how great its impiety.' At the same time he told her how himself, when a little one, had by his misguided mother been consigned over to the Manichees, and had not only read, but frequently copied out almost all their books, and had (without any argument or proof from any one) seen how much that sect was to be avoided; and had avoided it. Which when he had said, and she would not be satisfied, but urged him more with entreaties and many tears, that he would see me, and discourse with me; he being a little displeased at her importunity said, 'Go thy ways, and God bless thee, for it is not possible that the son of these tears should perish'" (*Confess.*, iii. 12).

Then Monica took up her hope again and awaited the return of her wandering child with confidence.

"For, almost nine years passed, in which I wallowed in the mire of that deep pit, and in the darkness of falsehood, often assaying to rise, but as often dashed down the more grievously. All which time that chaste, godly, and sober widow, (such as Thou lovest,) now more cheered with hope, yet no whit relaxing in her weeping and mourning, ceased not at all hours of her devotions to bewail my case unto Thee. And her *prayers entered into Thy presence*;[1] and notwithstanding Thou sufferedst me to be yet involved and reinvolved in that darkness" (*Confess.*, iii. 11).

At this time Augustine's zeal for Manicheism sustained a serious chill. It has before been noted that certain points of the doctrine perplexed him. He awaited with impatience the arrival of a celebrated bishop of the Manicheans at Carthage, Faustus, for he expected that this learned man would clear up all his doubts. He requested an interview with Faustus, but the result was not what he had hoped for. Faustus only gave evasive answers to all the questions he addressed to him, and Augustine's expectation was completely disappointed.

"When I had brought forward such things as perplexed me, I found him first utterly ignorant of the liberal sciences, save grammar, and that he knew but in an ordinary way. But because he had read some of Tully's orations, a very few books of Seneca, some things of the poets, and such few volumes of his own sect as were written in elegant Latin, and was daily practised in speaking, he acquired a certain eloquence, which proved the more pleasing and seductive for being under the guidance of a good wit, and accompanied with a kind of natural gracefulness" (*Confess.*, v. 6).

"When I put to him the difficulties which perplexed me, to be considered and discussed, he modestly shrunk from the burthen as beyond his powers. For

[1] Ps. lxxxviii. 1.

he knew that he knew not these things, and was not ashamed to confess it. For he was not one of those talking persons, many of whom I had endured, who undertook to teach me these things, and yet told me nothing. But this man had a heart, and though not right towards Thee, yet neither was he altogether treacherous to himself. For he was not altogether ignorant of his own ignorance, nor would he rashly be entangled in a dispute whence he could neither retreat nor extricate himself fairly. Even for this I liked him the better. For fairer is the modesty of a candid mind, than the knowledge of those things which I desired; and such I found him in all the more difficult and subtile questions. My zeal for the writings of Manicheans was thus blunted" (*Confess.*, v. 7).

That which still kept him with them was principally the error that he shared with them about the Divine Nature, besides the facility they offered him of laying his faults on a cause distinct from himself, this eternal principle of evil which disputed for the world with the principle of good, which he would fain persuade himself was a strange nature sinning in him (*Confess.*, v. 10).

He then began to think of leaving Carthage and going to teach in Rome; not that he was ambitious, but because he was weary of the licence of the Carthaginian students, and their rude, wild habits. "I did not wish therefore to go to Rome because higher gains and higher dignities were warranted me by my friends who persuaded me to this (though even these things had at that time an influence over my mind); but my chief and almost only reason was, that I heard that young men studied there more peacefully, and were kept quiet under a restraint of more regular discipline; so that they did not, at their pleasure, petulantly rush into the school of one whose pupils they were not, nor were they even admitted without his permission. Whereas at Carthage there reigns among the scholars a most disgraceful and unruly licence. They burst in audaciously, and with gestures almost frantic, disturb all the arrangements which are established for the good of the scholars. Divers outrages they commit with a wonderful stolidity, punishable by law, did not custom uphold them" (*Confess.*, v. 8).

But Augustine feared his mother's resistance, and the opposition of his protector Romanianus. He only disclosed his project to some friends who had encouraged him in it, and had decided to follow him. And when the hour of his departure was fixed he made his anxious mother believe that he was only going to say goodbye to a friend, who was waiting for a favourable wind to set sail. "And I lied to my mother, and to such a mother, and escaped; for, as she refused to return without me, I with difficulty persuaded her to stay that night in a place hard by our ship, where was an Oratory in memory of the blessed Cyprian. That night I privily departed, but she remained behind in weeping and prayer. And what, O Lord, was she with so many tears asking of Thee, but that Thou wouldst not suffer me to sail? But Thou in the depth of Thy counsels, and hearing the main point of her desire, regardedst not what she then asked, that Thou mightest make me what she ever asked. The wind blew and swelled our sails, and withdrew the shore from our sight; and she on the morrow was there, frantic with sorrow, and with complaints and groans filled Thine ears, who didst then disregard them; whilst through my desires, Thou wert hurrying me to quit those same desires" (*Confess.*, v. 8).

When he arrived in Rome, Augustine fell dangerously ill. They thought he was going to die, and to die without baptism. "And this my mother knew not, yet though absent prayed for me. But Thou everywhere present heardest her where she was; and where I was had compassion upon me, that I should recover the health of my body, though frenzied as yet in my sacrilegious heart. For I did not in all that danger desire Thy baptism; and I was better as a boy, when I begged it of my mother's piety, as I have before narrated and confessed. But I had grown up to my own shame, and I madly scoffed at the prescripts of Thy medicine, who wouldest not suffer me, being such, to die a double death. With such a wound had my mother's heart been pierced, it could never be healed. For I cannot express the affection she bare to me, and with how much more vehement anguish she was now in labour with me in the spirit, than at her child-bearing in the flesh.[1]

"I see not then how she should have been healed, had such a death of mine stricken through the bowels of her love. And where would have been those her so strong and unceasing prayers, un-

[1] Gal. iv. 19.

intermitting to Thee alone? But wouldest Thou, God of mercies, *despise the contrite and humbled heart*[1] of that chaste and sober widow, so frequent in alms-deeds, so full of duty and service to Thy saints, no day intermitting the oblation at Thine altar, twice a day, morning and evening, without any intermission coming to Thy Church, not for idle tattlings and *old wives' fables*;[2] but that she might hear Thee in Thy discourses, and Thou her in her prayers?" (*Confess.*, v. 9).

Having recovered his health, Augustine opened his school, and new pupils joined the disciples he had brought from Carthage. But here fresh disappointments awaited him. He was obliged to live by his lessons, and his scholars came to hear him willingly on condition that they had nothing to pay.

"I began then diligently to practise that for which I came to Rome, to teach rhetoric; and first to gather some to my house, to whom, and through whom I had begun to be known; when lo, I found other offences committed in Rome to which I was not exposed in Africa. True, those 'subvertings' by profligate young men were not here practised, as was told me; but on a sudden, to avoid paying their master's stipend, a number of youths would plot together, and remove to another;—breakers of faith who, for love of money, hold justice cheap" (*Confess.*, v. 12).

"When, therefore, they of Milan had sent to Rome to Symmachus, the prefect of the city, to furnish them with a rhetoric reader for their city, and send

---

[1] Ps. li. 17.   [2] 1 Tim. v. 10.

him at the public expense, I made application (through those very persons, intoxicated with Manichean vanities, to be freed wherefrom I was to go, neither of us however knowing it) that Symmachus, then prefect of the city, would try me by setting me some subject, and so send me" (*Confess.*, v. 13).

For two years he taught rhetoric at Milan; they admired his eloquence although he had a slight Carthaginian accent,[1] and on solemn occasions they always had recourse to him, when a panegyric on the emperor or some great person was to be delivered.

But if his self-love was satisfied, his soul, always enamoured of truth, made him feel the frivolity of such orations, and the vanity of such successes. He reproached himself with retailing lies, which were applauded even by those who knew that he lied, and for employing the science which he had acquired only to please men, instead of to instruct them (*Confess.*, vi. 6).

He then thought of seeking from platonic philosophy that truth which always eluded his pursuit. "After I had settled in Italy I entered, so to say, into conference with myself, in order to examine thoroughly, not if I should remain attached to the Manichean sect, to which I now regretted having pledged myself, but by what means I might arrive at the knowledge of that truth after which I ardently aspired" (*De util. cred.*, viii.).

---

[1] "Me enim ipsum adhuc, in multis sonis, Itali exagitant" (*De ordine*, ii. 17).

Victorinus, a celebrated professor of rhetoric at Rome, had just translated several works of Plato into Latin. Augustine read them eagerly, and little by little he felt the errors dispelled with which Manicheism had darkened his understanding. The idea that he was made out of God, according to their system, then appeared to him gross and full of contradictions. He at last understood that the Divine Nature necessarily excludes material form, however subtle it may be imagined, and also the rivalry of a principle independent of God, and disputing with Him from eternity the empire of the world. He understood and admired the doctrine of Greek philosophy, and light arose in his mind. What was the corporeal God of the Manicheans, imprisoned in matter, beside the sovereign good, the pure essence and ideal type of perfection, which Plato revealed to him in the following apostrophe:

" He who has reached the highest degree of initiation in the mysteries of love, will see suddenly appear before his sight a marvellous beauty, an eternal beauty, neither engendered, nor perishable, exempt from decay as from increase, which is not beautiful in one part and ugly in another, or beautiful for this person and ugly for that; a beauty which has no sensible form, no face or hands or anything of the body, which does not reside in any changing being, in animal or earth or sky, absolutely identical in itself, and invariable in its essence; in which all other beauties participate, without their birth or their destruction bringing it increase or diminution, or the slightest change. O, my dear Socrates, what gives worth to this life is the vision of Eternal Beauty. What a destiny is that of a mortal to whom it might be given to contemplate unalloyed beauty in its purity and simplicity, no longer clothed with flesh and human colour, and all these vain delights fated to perish, and to whom it should be given to see under its unique form—Divine Beauty!" (Plato, *Symposium*). Augustine's eyes were opened. Plato's doctrine seemed to him so close in certain points to evangelic wisdom, that he asked himself if the Greek philosopher had not had some knowledge of the Holy Books.

However, if the *Logos* of Plato, through which every creature shares some semblance of the divine being, seemed to recall to him the Word-mediator between man and God, it only revealed the Word in His Divinity; it showed neither the Word made man, or the Word as Redeemer. "I read in these books that the *Word*, who is God, is not born of the flesh, and that He is born of God. I did not read in them that the *Word* was made flesh, and dwelt among us. I only found there, that before all time, and beyond all time, Thine only Son eternally dwells, co-eternal with Thee, that it is of His fulness men receive happiness, and by participation in the wisdom that dwells in Him that they are renewed, and become holy. But it was not told that at the appointed time He came down and died for sinners; that Thou hast not spared Thine only Son, but hast delivered Him up for our salvation; for Thou hast hidden these things from the wise and revealed them unto babes, so that they who are burdened and heavy laden may come to Him, and that He may relieve them" (*Confess.*, vii. 9).

Thus, according to Augustine's confession, it was the platonic doctrine which opened his eyes, and prepared him to become a Christian; but at the same time it left in his soul a void which it could not fill. It revealed the true God to him, but without giving him the means of reaching this God, or of raising himself towards Him. It enlightened his obscured reason, but it was powerless to strengthen his will or to turn him to good.

"Then I sought a way of obtaining strength sufficient to enjoy Thee; and found it not until I embraced that Mediator between God and men, the Man Christ Jesus,[1] who is over all,—God blessed for evermore,[2] calling unto me, and saying, I am the Way, the Truth, and the Life,[3] and mingling that food which I was unable to receive, with our flesh. For the Word was made flesh,[4] that Thy wisdom, whereby Thou createdst all things, might provide milk for our infant state. For I did not hold to my Lord Jesus Christ humbling myself to the humble; nor knew I yet whereto His infirmity would guide us. For Thy Word, the Eternal Truth, far above the higher parts of Thy Creation, raises up the subdued unto Itself; but in this lower world built for Itself a lowly habitation of our clay, whereby to abase from themselves such as would be subdued, and bring them over to Himself; allaying their swelling, and fomenting their love; to the end they might

---

[1] 1 Tim. ii. 5. [2] Rom. ix. 5.
[3] John xiv. 6. [4] *Ib.* i. 14.

go on no further in self-confidence, but rather consent to become weak, seeing before their feet the Divinity weak by taking our *coats of skin* ;[1] and being wearied, might cast themselves down upon It, and It rising might lift them up" (*Confess.*, vii. 18).

The Greek philosopher showed him the temple of the true God; the Redeemer must bring him into it. "Plato gave me knowledge of the true God, Jesus Christ showed me the way."

Admonished by this doctrine to pull himself together, Augustine began to collect his thoughts and to disengage his reason from the tumult of the senses. "And being admonished by what I had read in these books to return to myself, I entered even into my inward self, Thou being my guide: and able I was for Thou wert become my Helper. And I entered and beheld with the eye of my soul (such as it was), above the same eye of my soul, above my mind, the Light Unchangeable. Not this ordinary light which all flesh may look upon, nor as it were a greater of the same kind, as though the brightness of this should be manifold brighter, and with its greatness take up all space. Nor was it above my soul as oil is above water, nor yet as heaven above earth, but above my soul because It made me; and I below It, because I was made by It" (*Confess.*, vii. 10).

Being disposed in such a way, Augustine profited even from the errors of the Academicians, who had wandered insensibly from the doctrine of their Masters, and had fallen into a semi-scepticism which

[1] Gen. iii. 21.

they called Probabilism.[1] The uncertainty, the diversity and the inconstancy of human life which had cast the Academicians into doubt, inclined Augustine on the contrary to religion, confirming him in the opinion that reason, however powerful it might be, could not suffice entirely for itself, and that what was wanting to it must be asked from a superior authority. (*De utilit. cred.*, viii.).

The reading of the Sacred Books, for which he was now ripe, was to finish the work begun by the philosophers.

"Upon these, I believe, Thou therefore willedst that I should fall, before I studied Thy Scriptures that it might be imprinted on my memory, how I was affected by them; and that afterwards when my spirits were tamed through Thy books and my wounds touched by Thy healing fingers I might discern and distinguish between presumption and confession; between those who saw whither they were to go, yet saw not the way; and the way that leadeth not to behold only but to dwell in that beatific country. For had I first been formed in Thy Holy Scriptures and hadst Thou in the familiar use of them grown sweet unto me, and had I then fallen upon those other volumes, they might perhaps have withdrawn me from the solid ground of piety, or had I continued in that healthful frame which I had thence imbibed I might have thought that it might have been obtained by the study of those books alone" (*Confess.*, vii. 20).

The divine seed having fallen on Augustine's soul,

---

[1] See Appendix.

the Bishop of Milan, Saint Ambrose, fertilised it. Augustine had seen nothing at first in the bishop's preaching but an oratorical display, which was worthy of interest to any man enamoured as he was of the talent of speech.

"To Milan I came to Ambrose, the bishop known to the whole world as among the best of men, Thy devout servant; whose eloquent discourse did then plentifully dispense unto Thy people the flour of Thy wheat, the gladness of Thy oil, and the sober inebriation of Thy wine.[1] To him was I unknowingly led by Thee, that by him I might knowingly be led to Thee. That man of God received me as a father, and showed me an episcopal kindness, on my coming. Thenceforth I began to love him, at first indeed not as a teacher of the truth (which I utterly despaired of in Thy Church), but as a person kind towards myself, and I listened diligently to him preaching to the people, not with that intent I ought, but, as it were, trying his eloquence, whether it answered the fame thereof, or flowed fuller or lower than was reported; and I hung on his words attentively; but of the matter I was as a careless and scornful looker-on; and I was delighted with the sweetness of his discourse, more recondite, yet in manner less winning and harmonious, than that of Faustus. Of the matter, however, there was no comparison; for the one was wandering amid Manichean delusions, the other teaching salvation most soundly. But salvation is far from sinners,[2] such as I then stood before him; and yet was I draw-

[1] Ps. iv. 7; civ. 15.   [2] Ps. cxix. 155.

ing nearer by little and little, and unconsciously. For though I took no pains to learn what he spake, but only to hear how he spake (for that empty care alone was left me, despairing of a way, open for man, to Thee); yet together with the words which I would choose came also into my mind the things which I would refuse; for I could not separate them. And while I open my heart to admit 'how eloquently he spake,' there also entered 'how truly he spake,' but this by degrees" (*Confess.*, v. 13, 14).

Augustine was particularly struck by the way in which the Bishop explained the difficult passages of the Scriptures to the people, showing under the letter which kills, the spirit which gives life; under the figures of the ancient law, the unveiled brightness of the new law; and in what a victorious manner he replied to the imputations with which the Manicheans had inspired their hearers against the Catholic Church. "I determined therefore so long to be a Catechumen in the Catholic Church, to which I had been commended by my parents, till something certain should dawn upon me, whither I might steer my course" (*Confess.*, v. 14).

It was the first step.

What hindered him from going further? What obstacle kept him back? He tells us with his habitual sincerity, and makes us spectators of the combat which was fought within him, by a sort of dramatic dialogue, between his soul, which no longer had serious doubts, and his half-healed heart. "So things in the ecclesiastical books are not absurd to us now, which sometimes seemed absurd, and may be otherwise taken, and in a good sense. I will take my stand, where as a child my parents placed me, until the clear truth be found out. But where shall it be sought or when? Ambrose has no leisure; we have no leisure to read; where shall we even find the books? Whence or when procure them? from whom borrow them? Let set times be appointed, and certain hours be ordered for the health of our soul. Great hope has dawned; the Catholic Faith teaches not what we thought and vainly accused it of; her instructed members hold it profane to believe God to be bounded by the figure of a human body: and do we doubt to 'knock' that the rest 'may be opened?' The forenoons our scholars take up; what do we during the rest? Why not this? But when then pay we court to our great friends whose favour we need? When compose what we may sell to scholars? When refresh ourselves unbending our minds from this intenseness of care?"

"Perish everything, dismiss we these empty vanities, and betake ourselves to the due search for truth! Life is vain, death uncertain; if it steals upon us on a sudden in what state shall we depart hence? And where shall we learn what here we have neglected? And shall we rather not suffer the punishment of this negligence? What if death itself cut off and end all care and feeling? Then must this be ascertained. But God forbid this! It is no vain and empty thing that the excellent dignity of the authority of the Christian Faith hath overspread the whole world. Never would such great things be by God wrought for us, if, with the death of the body, the life of the soul came to an end. Wherefore delay then to abandon worldly hopes and give ourselves wholly to seek after God and the blessed life" (*Confess.*, vi. 11).

Such was the voice of his reason once it had caught a glimpse of the light.

His heart alone, his rebellious heart, still murmured objections, counselled delay, and made "the aspirations of the age" honours, fortune, and a brilliant marriage glitter before his eyes. "But wait! Even those things are pleasant; they have some, and no small sweetness. We must not lightly abandon them, for it were a shame to return again to them. See, it is no great matter now to obtain some station, and then what should we more wish for? We have store of powerful friends; if nothing else offer, and we be in much haste, at least a presidentship may be given us; and a wife with some money, that she increase not our charges; and this shall be the bound of our desire. Many great men and most worthy of imitation have given themselves to the study of wisdom in the state of marriage" (*Confess.*, vi. 11).

Besides, it was Monica's wish to see Augustine married. She could not endure life separated from her son, so she left Africa and sailed for Italy, braving the storms and encouraging the terrified sailors, and joined Augustine at Milan, where she soon became acquainted with St Ambrose; he was struck with Monica's wonderful piety, and admired in her the marvellous union of divine with maternal love (*Confess.*, vi. 2).

Dreading her son's weakness, she wished him to

marry before receiving baptism. But first it was necessary to break the illegitimate tie which had bound him for so many years. The mother of Adeodatus, who had followed him to Milan, yielding to Monica's supplications, consented to separate from her son, and from Augustine; and it seems as if she, fortified by the example of Monica in making this painful sacrifice, had in view the salvation of the soul of her son, and of him whom she had loved so well, for when she left them to return to Africa she made a vow never to belong to another, and to consecrate herself to God in seclusion (*Confess.*, vi. 15).

Augustine had not the strength to follow her example, he fell again, reproaching himself for his base cowardice without having the power to overcome it (*Confess.*, vi. 15).

Alypius, his dearest and most faithful friend, besought him earnestly to live in chastity, and even dissuaded him from marriage, so that he could consecrate himself entirely to friendship and the worship of wisdom. Augustine thought it impossible for him to live in celibacy, and confessed to his friend that no doctrine allured him more than that of the Epicurean philosophy which makes our highest good consist in pleasure, if only he could have believed that the soul dies with the body, and thus escapes the responsibility of its sins (*Confess.*, vi. 16).

But the teachings of St Ambrose were never more to be effaced from his soul; and to drive away the phantoms which haunted his imagination, he re-read the Scriptures, particularly the epistles of

St Paul (*Confess.*, vii. 21). Then the idea struck him to go and see the holy priest Simplicianus, who was the spiritual father of Bishop Ambrose.

"To him I related the mazes of my wanderings. But when I mentioned that I had read certain books of the Platonists which Victorinus, sometime Rhetoric Professor of Rome (who had died a Christian as I heard), had translated into Latin, he testified his joy that I had not fallen upon the writings of other philosophers full of *fallacies and deceits, after the rudiments of this world*,[1] whereas the Platonists many ways led to the belief in God and His Word" (*Confess.*, viii. 2).

"Then he spoke of Victorinus himself and how that aged man, most learned and skilled in the liberal sciences, and who had read and weighed so many works of the philosophers, the instructor of so many noble senators, who also, as a monument of his excellent discharge of his office, had (which men of this world esteem a high honour) both deserved and obtained a statue in the Roman Forum; how he, to that age, a worshipper of idols and a partaker of the sacrilegious rites to which almost all the nobility of Rome were given up; even he now blushed not to be the child of Thy Christ, and the new-born babe of Thy fountain; submitting his neck to the yoke of humility, and subduing his forehead to the reproach of the Cross" (*Confess.*, viii. 2).

Augustine emerged from this interview full of desire to imitate Victorinus, but he again felt himself unsettled and disquieted. "But that new will

[1] Col. ii. 8.

which had began to be in me, freely to serve Thee and to wish to enjoy Thee, O God, the only assured pleasantness, was not yet able to overcome my former wilfulness, strengthened by age. Thus did my two wills, one new, and the other old, one carnal, the other spiritual, struggle within me; and by their discord undid my soul" (*Confess.*, viii. 5). "And the thoughts wherein I meditated on Thee were like the efforts of such as would awake, who, yet overcome with a heavy drowsiness, are again drenched therein" (*Confess.*, viii. 5).

"The very toys of toys, and vanities of vanities, my ancient mistresses, still held me; they plucked my fleshly garments, and whispered softly, 'Dost thou cast us off? and from that moment shall we no more be with thee forever? and from that moment shall not this or that be lawful for thee forever?' And what was it which they suggested in that I said, 'this or that,' what did they suggest, O my God? Let Thy mercy turn it away from the soul of Thy servant. And now I much less than half heard them, but muttering as it were behind my back, and privily plucking me to look back on them. Yet they did retard me, so that I hesitated to burst away and shake myself free from them, and to spring over whither I was called; a violent habit saying to me, 'Thinkest thou, thou canst live without them?'" (*Confess.*, viii. 11).

The decisive crisis was approaching. Augustine was living at Milan with his mother, his son, and certain friends who would not leave him, amongst these were Licentius, the son of Romanianus,

Nebridius, and Alypius. One day when he was alone with Alypius, a Christian, Pontitianus, came to visit him, and seeing the Epistles of St Paul on the table, he congratulated him on his taking delight in reading them. Then as the interview went on he spoke of Antony, the recluse of Thebais, who was known and revered by all Christians, and was astonished that his name had not reached them. "Thence his discourse turned to the flocks in the monasteries, and their holy ways, a sweet smelling savour unto Thee, and the fruitful deserts of the wilderness, whereof we knew nothing" (*Confess.*, viii. 6).

He related to them how two lords of the court, having by chance entered a hovel inhabited by a humble servant of God, had found there *A Life of Saint Antony*, and how having read it they were suddenly illuminated by grace, and being converted, had abandoned their titles and dignities to tread in the footprints of the holy anchorite (*Confess.*, viii. 6).

" But Thou, O Lord, while Pontitianus was speaking, didst turn me round towards myself, taking me from behind my back where I had placed me, unwilling to observe myself, and setting me before my face that I might see how foul I was, how crooked and defiled, bespotted, and ulcerous, and I beheld and stood aghast; and whither to flee from myself I found not. And if I sought to turn mine eye from off myself, he went on with his relation, and Thou again didst set me over against myself, and thrustedst me before my eyes, that I *might find out mine own iniquity, and hate it.*[1] I had known it, but made as though I saw it not, winked at it, and forgot it. . . . But I wretched, most wretched in the very commencement of my early youth, had begged chastity of Thee, and said, 'Give me chastity and continency, only not yet.' For I feared lest Thou shouldst hear me soon and soon cure me of the disease of concupiscence which I wished to have satisfied, rather than extinguished" (*Confess.*, viii. 7).

There was no longer any doubt; this was the last obstacle. Truth had appeared to him clearly, and he could not now allege his ignorance, or the uncertainty of his mind. "And I had thought that I therefore deferred from day to day to reject the hopes of this world and follow Thee only, because there did not appear aught certain whither to direct my course, but now the truth was certain, and I still continued to bear the burden" (*Confess.*, viii. 7).

Pontitianus went away, and Augustine full of trouble and agitation suddenly exclaimed to the astonished Alypius: "What ails us? what is it, what heardedst thou? The unlearned start up and take heaven by force,[2] and we with our learning, and without heart, lo, where we wallow in flesh and blood" (*Confess.*, viii. 8). And whilst the passions still muttered round him, he seemed to see Chastity, with a train of young men and maidens, a multitude of youth and every age, grave widows and aged virgins, and she smiled on him with a persuasive

[1] Ps. xxxvi. 2.   [2] Matt. vi. 12.

mockery as would she say, "Canst thou not what these youths, what these maidens can?" (*Confess.*, viii. 11).

They both sat down in the little garden, Alypius silent, respecting the trouble of friend, Augustine striking his breast, his soul torn by the violent struggle, and a prey to the most cruel anguish. At last, unable to master his emotion, he moved a few steps away that he might be able to weep more freely. When he was alone he prostrated himself under a fig-tree, and with floods of tears, addressed to God his fervent supplications.

Suddenly he heard a childish voice which seemed to come from a neighbouring house, singing over and over again, "Take and read, take and read." He asked himself if this could be the refrain of some child's game, but, not being able to recall anything of the sort, he remembered that Saint Antony entering a church at the moment when they were reading this verse of the Gospel, " Sell all that you have and give to the poor, and you shall have treasure in heaven, and come and follow Me," had seen in these words a divine admonition, and had immediately consecrated himself to God. Persuaded that the voice which he had just heard was from Heaven, he rose and returned to the place where he had left Alypius, took the Epistles of St Paul, and opened them at this verse: " Not in rioting and drunkenness, *not in chambering and wantonness, not in strife and envying: but put ye on the Lord Jesus Christ, and make not provision for the flesh* [1] in concupiscence " (*Confess.*, viii. 12).

[1] Rom. xiii. 13, 14.

"No further would I read; nor needed I; for instantly at the end of this sentence by a light, as it were, of serenity infused into my heart, all the darkness of doubt vanished away.

"Then putting my finger between or some other mark, I shut the volume, and with a calmed countenance made it known to Alypius. And what was wrought in him, which I knew not, he thus shewed me. He asked to see what I had read; I shewed him; and he looked even further than I had read, and I knew not what followed. This followed, '*him that is weak in the faith receive;*'[1] which he applied to himself and disclosed to me. And by this admonition was he strengthened; and by a good resolution and purpose, and most corresponding to his character, wherein he did always very far differ from me for the better, without any turbulent delay he joined me. Thence we go into my mother; we tell her; she rejoices; we relate in order how it took place; she leaps for joy, and triumphs, and blesses Thee, *Who art able to do above that which we ask or think;*[2] for she perceived that Thou hadst given her more for me than she was wont to beg by her pitiful and most sorrowful groanings. For Thou convertedst me unto Thyself, so that I sought neither wife, nor any hope of this world, standing in that rule of faith where Thou hadst shewed me unto her in a vision, so many years before" (*Confess.*, viii. 12).

It was the month of September and the term was just at an end. Augustine did not wish to reascend "this pulpit of lies," and announced that he would

---

[1] Rom. xiv. 1.   [2] Eph. iii. 20.

not resume his teaching. His voice was weakened by fatigue, and he was glad that this ailment furnished him with a valid reason for giving up his work without annoying those who had conferred the post on him or those to whom he lectured.

A friend of Nebridius, a professor like himself, had a country house, known under the name of Cassiaciacum, in the suburbs of Milan. He offered it to Augustine who retired there with his mother, his brother Navigius, his son Adeodatus, his cousins, Alypius "the brother of his heart," Licentius, and some other friends (*Confess.*, ix. 3).

He stayed about seven months at Cassiaciacum preparing for his baptism, where they lived a community life under Monica's wise direction. They discussed various questions, walking in the country if it was fine, and in the hall of the bath if it was wet. Augustine wished his mother to take part in these discussions as he admired the justness of her mind. "There have been many philosophical women in antiquity, he said to her, but your philosophy pleases me more than any of theirs." And Monica replied with gentle humility that he had never uttered so many lies (*De Ordine*, i. 11).

One day his mother came in as he was talking with his friends of the harmony and power of numbers, and Augustine, interrupting himself, said to her, "For you my mother whose genius appears new to me every day, and whose soul, through the effect of advancing years and admirable moderation, rises day by day above the region of vain and frivolous things, do these questions seem as easy to you as they are difficult for coarse minds who live in a carnal manner" (*De Ordine*, ii. 22).

Another time speaking of Providence, just as he was about to thank God whose goodness watches over children, he stopped and said to his mother, "That these prayers and wishes may be expressed with more fervour, we charge you with them, my mother. . . . And I firmly believe that having obtained for me the grace of ardently desiring the truth, you will yet obtain for me the grace of possessing it in fulness" (*De Ordine*, ii. 20).

One is always surprised when reading the account of the conversations and lectures at Cassiciacum, to see the place which the profane studies of poetry, rhetoric, and grammar hold in them; one would rather have expected from these new converts, from these penitents, the study and meditation of the Sacred Books. One of the speakers, Licentius, is a poet; Augustine defines him, a sort of bird who flutters incessantly and never rests in one place. He composes a poem on the adventures of Pyramis and Thisbe. Then philosophy intervenes in a debate; he declares that philosophy has made him forget the Muses, that she is more beautiful than Thisbe, and has greater attractions than Venus or Cupid. The memories of pagan antiquity mingle incessantly with Christian ideas; the speakers imitate Plato conversing with his disciples in the gardens of Academus, or Cicero debating with his friends under the shades of Tusculum.

The slightest incident becomes a point of departure

for a discussion or a digression. Thus the sound of a stream which runs behind the baths, and whose murmur is sometimes soft, sometimes loud, furnishes Augustine with an argument for demonstrating the order which Providence has established in the universe, this inequality in the murmur of the water proceeding from the fall of the leaves of a tree into the stream. "Let us remark in these two cocks with their heads erect and threatening, their bristling plumage, and the violence of the blows they give each other, the adroitness with which they parry them, and in all the movements of these creatures without reason, an order which I can hardly describe, but which pleases one, because it shows a superior reason which presides, even at this combat. Who would not admire the glory of the victor? the pride of his crowing, with his limbs puffed out like a wheel, witnessing his victory; and perceive the sad marks of defeat in the walk and voice of the vanquished. Thus, all this together, has a sort of beauty in its exact relation to the laws of nature, even the humiliation of the vanquished, though painful to see, co-operating in the gratification of the combat" (*De Ordine*, i. 8).

One might from all this be tempted to believe that profane philosophy and literature still held in Augustine's soul the same rank as before his conversion. But when one looks closer, one observes that Augustine, living in the midst of literary people whom he wished to convert or strengthen in the faith, wished to show them that the Christian religion exacted from them neither the sacrifice of their reason, nor the proscription of eloquence or pagan poetry. And from these conversations which he directed he always strove to draw some edifying deduction, which the subject itself, or some incident during the discussion, brought forward. Thus one day when Trigetius had expressed a false opinion, and through vanity did not wish it to be reproduced by the stenographer, while Licentius jealously insisted that it should be mentioned, Augustine immediately brought them back to humility and Christian charity. " Is this how you act? Is this that raising of yourselves towards God which I believed you had reached, this love of truth which rejoiced me? Oh, if you could see, even with my feeble eyes, the ugliness and madness of the evil this joy reveals, with what haste you would change it into floods of tears. . . . Do not grieve me any more in this way, if it is true that you owe me some tenderness, if you understood how much I love you, how full I am with the care of forming your manners! You take a pleasure in calling me your master; I only ask one single recompense from you: Be good men!" (*De Ordine*, i. 10).

The three dialogues which Augustine has drawn from these conversations—*Against the Academicians, Of the Happy Life*, and *Of Order*—show the preoccupations of the Christian and of the neophyte, which appear incessantly under the literary man and the philosopher. The dialogue, *Against the Academicians*, dedicated to his protector Romanianus, is not alone a refutation of the semi-scepticism of the Academy; it ends in this conclusion, that the soul cannot live in uncertainty, and content itself in wandering in the pursuit of truth; that it cannot find peace of mind except in the possession of truth; that no philosopher gives it to us, and that we can only receive it from the Divine Word (*Contra Academicos*, ii. 29).

The dialogue, *The Happy Life*, differs little apparently from the treatise of Seneca on the same subject. Like the stoic philosopher Augustine makes happiness consist in the equilibrium of the soul; but this equilibrium the Christian alone can establish in himself; peace for the soul can be found in God only. He alone can satisfy it; and Monica is transported with joy, recognising in this definition the beatitude at which one arrives "guided by faith, borne by hope, sustained by charity" and in her joy she intones the hymn, *Fove peccantes, Trinitas* (*De Vita Beata*, xxxv.).

The dialogue on *Order* shows that by the chastisement of the hardened sinner and the mercy granted to the repentant one, Providence maintains order and harmony in the moral world of which the concert is destroyed by sin (*De Ordine*, i. 8).

Augustine was to receive baptism on Easter Day, so they left Cassiciacum to return to Milan; his son Adeodatus and his friend Alypius were baptised with him the night of the 24th or 25th of April 387. "We joined with us the boy Adeodatus, born after the flesh, the son of my sin. Excellently hadst Thou made him. He was not then quite fifteen, and in wit surpassed many grave and learned men. I confess unto Thee Thy gifts, O Lord, my God,

Creator of all, and abundantly able to reform our deformities: for I had no part in that boy but the sin. For that we brought him up in Thy discipline, it was Thou, none else, had inspired us with it" (*Confess.*, ix. 6).

But Adeodatus was to be taken from him shortly afterwards, and the grief of this loss was softened for Augustine by the thought that this cherished son would escape those disorders from which his father had not known how to preserve himself. "Soon didst Thou take his life from the earth: and I now remember him without anxiety, fearing nothing for his childhood or youth, or his whole self. Him we joined with us, our contemporary in grace, to be brought up in Thy discipline: and we were baptised, and anxiety for our past life vanished from us" (*Confess.*, ix. 6).

It was St Ambrose who baptised them, and remembering the words of the Gospel, "There is more joy in Heaven for one sinner that does penance than for ninety and nine just persons who need no repentance" (St Luke xv. 7), he thanked God for this marvellous conversion. "When one sees a man who has fallen into licentiousness in his youth, change his life at an advanced age, come to wash away his sins in the waters of baptism, renounce his past life, tear his evil habits from him, and ask to be buried with Jesus Christ, so that the world may be crucified for him, and he to the world, does it not seem that this man may have more glory and be a greater cause of rejoicing to the Church than he who has always led an innocent life before his baptism?" The holy bishop knew that it is more difficult to overcome the habit of evil, and to regain possession of the will when it has lost the power of resisting the passions, than to follow in the right way where one has never wandered from it.

Now that he was a Christian, Augustine only thought of returning to Africa to live there in seclusion and consecrate the rest of his life to God. They went to Ostia where they were to embark, and it was there that Augustine had a last colloquy with his mother, who was not again to see Africa. They were alone, leaning at a window, the view from which extended over the garden of the house they occupied, and the mouth of the Tiber. They were talking together with an infinite sweetness of what eternal happiness must be. "And when our discourse was brought to that point, that the very highest delight of the earthly senses, in the very purest material light, was, in respect of the sweetness of that life, not only not worthy of comparison, but not even of mention, we raising up ourselves with a more glowing affection towards the 'Self-same,' did by degrees pass through all things bodily, even the very heaven whence sun and moon and stars shine upon the earth; yea, we were soaring higher yet, by inward musing and discourse and admiring of Thy works; and we came to our own minds and went beyond them, that we might arrive at that region of never-failing plenty, where *Thou feedest Israel*[1] for ever with the food of truth,

[1] Ps. lxxx. 1.

and where life is the *wisdom by whom all these things are made*, that have been and that shall be; and She is not made, but is as She hath been, and so shall She be for ever; yea rather, to 'have been,' and 'hereafter to be' are not in Her, but only 'to be' seeing She is eternal. And while we were discoursing and panting after Her, we slightly touched on Her with the whole effort of our heart; and we sighed and there we left bound, *the first fruits of spirit*[1] and returned to vocal expressions of our mouth, where the word spoken has beginning and end. And what is like unto Thy Word, our Lord, who endureth in himself without becoming old, and *maketh all things new*?[2]

"We were saying then: If to any the tumult of the flesh were hushed, hushed the images of earth, and waters, and air, hushed also the poles of heaven, yea, the very soul be hushed to herself, and by not thinking on self surmount self, hushed all dreams and imaginary revelations, every tongue and every sign, and whatsoever exists only in transition, since if any could hear all these say, We made not ourselves, but He made us, that abideth for ever. If then, having uttered this, they too should be hushed, having roused only our ears to Him who made them, and He alone speak, not by them, but by Himself, that we may hear His word, not through any tongue of flesh, nor angel's voice, nor sound of thunder, nor in the dark riddle of a similitude, but might hear whom in these things we love, might hear His very self without these (as we two now strained ourselves,

[1] Rom. viii. 23. [2] Wisdom vii. 27.

and in swift thought touched on that Eternal Wisdom, which abideth over all); could this be continued on, and other visions of kind far unlike be withdrawn, and this one ravish and absorb and wrap up its beholder amid these inward joys, so that life might be for ever like that one moment of understanding which now we sighed after; were not this, *Enter into thy Master's joy*?[1] And when shall that be? When *we shall all rise again*, though we shall not all be changed.[2]

"Such things was I speaking, and even if not in this very manner, and these same words, yet, Lord, Thou knowest that in that day when we were speaking of these things, and this world with all its delights became as we spake contemptible to us, my mother said: 'Son, for mine own part, I have no further delight in anything in this life. What I do here any longer, and to what end I am here, I know not, now that my hopes in this world are accomplished. One thing there was for which I desired to linger for a while in this life, that I might see thee a Catholic Christian before I died. My God hath done this for me more abundantly, that I should now see thee withal, despising earthly happiness, become His servant; what do I here?'" (*Confess.*, ix. 10).

Five days after, as if God had wished to grant her prayer, she fell sick and died. Having recovered consciousness at the moment of death, she said to her sons, who could scarcely restrain their tears: "You will bury your mother here." Augustine was silent, but his brother expressed regret that she

---

[1] Matt. xxv. 21.   [2] 1 Cor. xv. 51, Vulg.

might not die in her own country. "Lay," she saith, "this body anywhere; let not the care for that any way disquiet you; this only I request, that you would remember me at the Lord's altar wherever you be" (*Confess.*, ix. 11).

Some time before, a friend of Augustine's had asked her if it would not be a grief to her to be buried in a land so far from her own, and she replied, "One is never far from God" (*Confess.*, ix. 11).

"O Lord, my God," cries St Augustine, finishing this painful story, " inspire Thy servants, my brethren, Thy sons my masters, whom with voice and heart and pen I serve; that so many as shall read these Confessions may at Thy altar remember Monica Thy handmaid, with Patricius, her sometime husband, by whose bodies Thou broughtest me into this life, how, I know not. May they with devout affection remember my parents in this transitory light, my brethren under Thee, our Father in our Catholic mother, and my fellow citizens in that eternal Jerusalem which Thy pilgrim people sigheth after from their Exodus, even unto their return thither; that so my mother's last request of me may, through my Confessions more than through my prayers, be, through the prayers of many, more abundantly fulfilled to her" (*Confess.*, ix. 13).

Monica might die, for her work was accomplished; she had attained the only aim of her life, she had re-conquered for God the soul of her well-beloved son; and this son, thrilled with gratitude, never ceased repeating that his marvellous and unhoped-for conversion was due only to the piety, the persevering faith, and the ardent prayers of his mother. One finds impressed on each page of his works, this humble and tender avowal: "It is through the merits of my mother that I possess the true life" (*De beata vita*).

"If I have not perished for ever in error and evil, it is because the tears of my mother, her persevering, faithful tears, have obtained this grace for me" (*De dono perseverantiæ*, xx. 53).

"I proclaim that it is thanks to the prayers of my mother, that God granted me to prefer Truth before all, to wish nothing, to seek nothing, to love nothing but Her" (*De ordine*, ii. 20).

So the liturgies of the religious orders who follow the rule of St Augustine celebrate above all, in the office of the feast of St Monica, the devotion of the Christian mother, and the victory obtained by her prayers and tears, as one can see in the following anthem:

"The tender mother wept and prayed unceasingly over this son, by whose hand the Lord has crushed the heads of the impious.

"O happy mother! who saw her desires fully granted, when, weeping over her son, she besought the Lord humbly.

"Thou hast heard, Lord, and Thou hast not despised the torrents of tears, which fell on the earth for the salvation of her son.

"Such was this widow, truly afflicted, who wept so long and so bitterly for her son.

"And the voice of these floods of tears shed by

his mother ascended unto Thee, Lord" (*Breviar. canonic. regul. Ordin. S. Augustini*, 1523).

And when the remains of St Monica were transported to Rome, the Sovereign Pontiff, Martin V., recalled in these touching words what St Augustine had owed to his holy mother: "We are celebrating to-day the mother of this great doctor, whose virtue, graces, and victories are the glory of all Christians, and whose name is celebrated amongst all people in the Catholic Church, and everywhere where the Faith reigns. Now, how can we exclude the mother from the praises which we lavish on the son, when none of us are unaware that the most happy Monica was not only his mother according to nature, but that she was still more the mother of his mind and heart. Indeed, the only aim of the prayers that she sent up every moment to God, the only object of her solicitude, was the salvation of Augustine. And he himself tells us in his writings that his mother said to him constantly, that she craved no other joy on earth, than to see her son inflamed at last with the desire of heavenly things, and despising the delights of earth."

"St Monica," says St Francis de Sales, "battled with the evil inclinations of her son with such vigour and confidence, that, having followed him by land and sea, she had more happiness in making him the child of her tears by the conversion of his soul, than in making him the child of her flesh in the bearing of his body" (*Introduction à la vie dévote*, 1st part, 38).

Augustine returned to Rome after the death of his

mother. He stayed there for some time, working for the conversion of those friends whom he had formerly led astray by his errors, and he began to write against heretics. He did not go back to Africa till the end of the summer of 388, and, before retiring to Thagaste, he stopped for some time at Carthage, then re-entered his native town and lived an altogether new life with his friends. Keeping barely what was necessary, he sold everything else, and distributed the money to the poor. He finished several works in this retreat that he had begun at Rome. "The Morals of the Catholic Church, and the Morals of the Manicheans," "The Book of the Master," "The Commentary on Genesis" against the Manicheans, and "The Treatise on the True Religion," which converted Romanianus, and which Antoine Arnauld translated in 1647, and prefaced by this glowing homage: "The perusal hereof will sufficiently set forth his excellence, and I believe that no other subject will so well show the grandeur of mind and the extraordinary insight of this incomparable man. For who must not marvel that he, so lately come to the knowledge of the Christian religion, and having as yet no other rank in the Church than that of a simple disciple, should be able to speak in such a noble and exalted way of this divine religion which a God Himself came to establish on the earth? And who will not form a high idea of his eminence and grandeur, finding that it is no slight thing to follow the flight of this eagle, to penetrate the solidity of his admirable reasonings, and to contemplate the high truths which he proposes, without being dazzled by such a shining light."

Augustine, through humility, believing himself unworthy, never dared to aspire to the priesthood, for which he seemed designed by his science and virtue. He carefully avoided those places where a bishop was to be appointed, knowing the rumours which in spite of him were attached to his name.

" I did everything I could to work out my salvation in a humble retreat, fearing to put myself in peril by standing in high positions. One day I went to Hippo, where I had a friend whom I had hopes of gaining for God and attaching to our community, and I went there without distrust as the town of Hippo had a bishop" (*Serm.*, 49).

He did not know that the Church of Hippo wanted a priest. They knew that Augustine was in the town, and the faithful in spite of his resistance dragged him before the Bishop Valerius, and unanimously demanded that he should be ordained. He tried in vain to screen himself from it. "You wish my ruin, then, my father Valerius. Where is your charity? Do you love me? Do you love the Church? How can you wish that one in my condition should serve her? Doubtless you do love her, and you love me also, I know; but you believe me fit for the sacred ministry, while I know myself better." He asked at least for some time to prepare himself by prayer and recollection (*Epist.*, xxi.) He was ordained priest at the age of thirty-seven, in 395.

Valerius gave him a garden near the church, where he established a sort of monastery. He lived there "after the rule of the holy apostles" with Alypius,

Evodius, Severus, Possidius, Fortunatus, and several other servants of God, called like himself to govern the churches of Africa. Here he finished "The Treatise on Free Will," composed the book "On the advantage of Belief," addressed to Honoratus; wrote the "Treatise on the Two Souls"—a reply to the Manicheans, and had a conference with Fortunatus, one of their priests, in which his adversary was publicly confounded. He began the struggle against the encroaching heresy of the Donatists, who pretended, as the Novatians did formerly, to repeat the baptism of the Catholic Church, whose validity they attacked, and to refuse absolution to certain sins, which they pronounced unpardonable; so that Augustine was charged to give a lecture on *Faith* and the *Creed*, at the General Council of all Africa, held at Hippo under the presidentship of Aurelius, Bishop of Carthage, in the presence of all the primates. The old Bishop Valerius then asked to have Augustine as a coadjutor, who, after having defended himself for a long time against this honour, received episcopal ordination a little before the feast of Christmas, 395. The death of Valerius soon after left him the only bishop of Hippo, and for thirty-five years, in spite of delicate health, he gave himself boldly, with an indefatigable activity and devotion, to the direction of souls, to the preaching of the holy word, to the defence of the Christian religion against the pagans, and to the incessant struggle against the heresies which were arising on all sides against the Catholic Church, as well by speech, in disputations where he was always ready to come forward, as by writings, whose penetrating eloquence, vigorous dialectic, and inexhaustible richness, we cannot sufficiently admire.

At one time it was the Manicheans, who were again raising their heads, and whom he was never weary of combating, refuting one by one the allegations of Faustinus, disputing with Felix in the Church of Hippo, and bringing him back to Catholicism; writing a new book against "The Letter of the Foundation"—a *resumé* of the errors of the sect, but always full of courtesy and indulgence towards individuals.

"Those may be irritated against you who have not fallen into your errors. For me who have swung backwards and forwards so long, and have at last reached the knowledge of this truth which does not admit a mixture of vain fables; for me who have hardly merited to be delivered from your imaginations, your systems, and your errors; who have responded so tardily to the pressing invitations of the gentlest of physicians to extricate my spirit from the darkness; for me who have wept so long that it might be given me to believe in the immutable and pure substance of which the divine books speak; who have sought with so much curiosity, listened with so much attention, believed with so much rashness, preached with so much ardour, defended with so much obstinacy all these dreams which enchant and captivate you,—for me, I should not know how to be irritated with you. It is my duty to bear with you to-day, as others bore with me in the day of my errors. I ought to have the same patience towards you as my friends had for me whilst I wandered, blinded and maddened in your belief.

Later, it was the Donatists, who pretended to supersede the Catholic Church, and who, not content with infecting with their false doctrines nearly every diocese in Africa, proceeded to the utmost excesses, had recourse to violence against their adversaries, committed many cruelties, and, furious at never being able to resist the victorious arguments of Augustine, preached publicly that to kill him would be a real service rendered to religion, and even went so far as to hire assassins to attempt his life.

Yet when the emperors promulgated severe laws against them, Augustine interceded for these culprits, and only employed against them the arms of gentleness and persuasion. The Emperor Honorius having obliged them to accept a public discussion at Carthage, St Augustine triumphed over them so brilliantly that at the end Honorius banished their clergy from Africa, and ordered their churches to be given up to the Catholics. Some of them refused to yield, and were menaced with severe penalties, but Augustine asked and obtained their pardon. "We do not accuse them, we do not persecute them; we should be grieved that the sufferings of the servants of God should be punished by the law of retaliation."

Finally, it was the votaries of Pelagius, a monk of Bangor in Wales, and his disciple Celestius, who pretended that the free-will of man dwelt inviolate in the children of Adam, and that they could by their own powers work out their salvation. This heresy aimed at nothing less than declaring the Incarnation of Jesus Christ and the Redemption useless, that is to say, at destroying the foundation of Christianity.[1]

The struggle was long and difficult. Condemned in the West by Pope Innocent, in accordance with the Synod of Carthage, where Augustine had stigmatised their doctrine as antichristian, Pelagius and Celestius, being excommunicated, sought refuge in the East, after having vainly had recourse to equivocal declarations, whose imposture Augustine unmasked. They were reproached for holding that man has no need of grace or of the help of God to effect his salvation; they replied that they believed the help of God was necessary to man; but when the full meaning of their doctrine was brought out, it was discovered that by this help of God they meant, not grace, but the gift of free-will, which in their eyes rendered grace useless.

Augustine's zeal followed them into Asia; he continued to combat them by lectures and writings; and he raised up a formidable adversary against them in the person of his friend Orosius. The Council of Diospolis, imposed upon by their ambiguous declarations, having declared them orthodox, Augustine again exposed the sophisms with which they had enveloped their heresies to seduce the Bishop of Cesarea; and their excommunication was confirmed by the Pope Innocent.

Pelagius did not consider himself vanquished; he circumvented Zozimus, Innocent's successor; but the bishops of Africa reunited in a general council at

[1] See Appendix.

Carthage, and the dangerous heresy of Pelagius was so clearly established there that Zozimus also condemned him, and the emperor banished both Pelagius and Celestius from his empire. After the death of Honorius and Zozimus, they came back to Italy and tried new and unavailing measures with the Pope Celestine. Then they went back to the East, and their hopes revived when Nestorius took possession of the See of Constantinople; but the Pope issued a fresh sentence against them; the Emperor Theodosius II. expelled them from Constantinople, and the third œcumenical council held at Ephesus pronounced against them a definite condemnation.

Augustine might believe the struggle ended:—"Two councils," he said to the faithful in his church, "have sent their decrees to the Apostolic See, and they have been confirmed by it. The trial is ended, may the error be ended also!" (*Serm.*, 132). But the error was going to reappear under the attenuated form of semi-Pelagianism. Augustine was informed that Cassien of Marseilles, and several monks of Lerins, refused to admit his doctrine on grace, holding that it was destructive of free-will, and affirming that our will, even though enfeebled as a consequence of original sin, preceded Divine Grace; that the first step towards good and the beginning of faith was the work of man, and influenced God to give him the necessary assistance to work out his salvation; and even that the perseverance necessary for salvation was the work of our own merits, and not of grace. Augustine replied by two treatises. "On the Predestination of the Saints," and "On the Gift of Perseverance," for he found that the bishops of Gaul were too slow in refuting this disguised Pelagianism. He had not much trouble in establishing that the new doctrine, without enunciating the principle of Pelagius, implied that to attribute to the creature and his own merits the initiative and perseverance in good, was really to subordinate Divine Grace to human liberty. The doctrine of the semi-Pelagians was condemned by the Councils of Orange and Valencia, and Pope Boniface II. confirmed their decision.

But the Church had not only to struggle with heresy, she had to defend herself against paganism. The Barbarians were invading the provinces; Alaric had pillaged Rome; the pagans accused the new religion of being the cause of their disasters, and imputed the calamities of the Empire to the anger of their gods, who had been outraged by the Christians. "When we offered sacrifices to our gods Rome was fortunate; now that our sacrifices are forbidden, see what Rome has become" (*Serm.*, 296). In his diocese Augustine replied to these blasphemies by preaching, but it was not sufficient; he wished to reply for the whole world, pagan and Christian, and he composed his beautiful book, "The City of God." Augustine returned the reproaches with which the pagans assailed the disciples of Jesus Christ. They imputed the disasters of Rome to the Christians, whereas it was owing to them that they were less terrible than they might have been. If Alaric had not annihilated the city, it was because being a Christian he respected the churches which served as refuges; the Barbarians spared pagans and Christians out of respect for Jesus Christ, whilst, during heathen times, the divinities of Troy were not only powerless to avert her fall, but the conquerors plundered their temples, and slaughtered the vanquished at the foot of their altars. The laws of war under which Rome suffered to-day had she not applied pitilessly since her beginning? And however great was the misfortune which now overwhelmed her, had she not experienced still more terrible ones during the course of her history, from which her gods had not preserved her, or done anything to deliver her in the hour of danger? They urge the recent misfortunes which have come on the Christians themselves, and the violence of which they have been victims, without their God having spread His shield over them; but in this life God allows misfortunes to fall equally on good and bad, and when He afflicts those who are faithful to Him, it is to prove their virtue, or to punish their faults. In exchange for their afflictions, if they accept them with resignation and endure them with piety, He reserves an eternal reward. Besides, what is this prosperity of Rome for which they do honour to their gods? If these gods had had the will or the power to assure the happiness of the Romans, they would before all have endowed them with virtue. What have they done to make them better or to regulate their morals, so as to preserve them from corruption? They say they have helped them to conquer the world? "To make war on one's neighbours and to subjugate peoples from whom one has received no provocation in order to satisfy one's ambition, can it be called anything but brigandage? Jesus Christ is drawing His own by degrees from this tottering world which He abandons to its fall, that He may establish an eternal city, whose glory is not founded like that of Rome on the vain praise of the world, but on eternal truth. Let the descendants of Regulus, Scaevola, Fabricius, instead of lamenting over the inevitable ruin of the Roman fatherland enter the Christian country; let them renounce the empire of the earth to gain the empire of Heaven. It is not chance; it is not gods of wood and stone, who have made the power of Rome; it is the Providence of the true God who establishes the kingdoms of the earth. The terrestial power of Rome has been the reward of the terrestial virtues of the ancient Romans. Since God could not grant them His eternal Kingdom, it was just that He should give them the glory of a temporal kingdom. They had merited human glory which passes away; and they obtained it. This perishable greatness rendered them neither better nor wiser than those they had vanquished. They have conquered earth, let them now try to conquer heaven. God made for Himself since the birth of time, two cities, one earthly and one heavenly, which here below are mingled but must one day be separated. Two loves have built these two cities; the heavenly one was built by love of God, the earthly one by love of self.

In reviewing the history of the world, Augustine

ascribes it altogether to this principle of Christian philosophy, which makes him perceive the counsel and action of Providence in every event.

However, the Vandals, who were Arians, and already masters of Spain, threatened the province of Africa. Count Boniface, who commanded the armies of the Empire in Africa, had wished to retire from the world after the death of his wife, but Augustine and Alypius, believing that he could serve the Empire and the Church more effectually in his position as commandant, had turned his thoughts away from the idea. He was sent to Spain by the emperor, and there he allowed himself to be enticed by an Arian lady, a relation of the king of the Vandals, and he married her. He became by this alliance an object of suspicion to the Empress Placidia, therefore he allied himself with the King Genseric, king of the Vandals, and attacked and routed the armies sent against him by the regent. Augustine then wrote him a letter in which he besought him to return to his duty. "Listen to me, my dear son, or rather listen to God, who speaks by my mouth; summon up your remembrances. What were the feelings of your heart during the last days of the life of your first wife of pious memory? You had a horror of the vanities of the world, and you wished to consecrate yourself entirely to the service of God. You say that your reasons for acting as you have done are just; I cannot decide, not having heard both parties, but whatever may be your reasons, which it is not necessary to examine at this moment, can you deny before God that what has impelled you to act as you have done, is the love of the goods of this world, which should be despised by a true servant of Jesus Christ, such as you were when you left us? What must I not say to you of the desolation of Africa? When you were only a tribune with a small number of confederates, you so terrified the Barbarians that they no longer dared to attempt anything, and who would not have been sure that when you were in Africa with the authority of a count and the command of a large body of troops, you would have kept the Barbarians at a distance, and even made them tributaries of the Empire? How far we are from these hopes. But enough, you will say more to yourself than we can say to you.

"You will doubtless reply that these ills must be attributed to those who have offended you, and rendered evil for your good. Instead of considering your relations with other men, examine what has passed between God and you. When I seek the cause of the calamities of Africa, I raise myself above your quarrels with those of whom you think you have reason to complain. I only lay the blame on the sins of men; but I could wish that you were not one of the instruments of God's justice here below, for to such He reserves eternal punishments if they do not amend themselves. Turn your thoughts then to God and to Jesus Christ, who has done so much even for those from whom He has only received injuries. I have not to examine which side has been the aggressor. I address myself to a Christian." (*Epist.*, ccxx.).

Touched by this letter Boniface lent himself to a reconciliation with Placidia, to which Augustine contributed his influence, but he could not hinder Genseric and the Vandals from invading Africa. The Barbarians carried desolation everywhere. Boniface tried in vain to stop them; his army was beaten, he was forced to shut himself up in Hippo, and the conquerors besieged the town.

Augustine did not allow himself to be cast down. The two bishops Quodvultdeus and Honoratus having consulted him as to what their conduct should be, the last alleging that Jesus Christ Himself had fled, and that He permitted flight, Augustine replied that a priest or a bishop may think of his own safety when the danger threatens only him, and when his people are not menaced; but that when the same misfortunes threaten the priest and the faithful, it is the pastor's duty to watch over his flock to the end, and he will commit a crime if he abandons it; that in such circumstances they had a great mission to fulfil, in raising the courage of the people, consoling the afflicted, sustaining those whose faith might be shaken, and dispensing priestly succour to all. He himself set the example, attending without relaxation to the work of God, fulfilling his duties as citizen and priest, though in danger from the Barbarians, forgetting himself, and thinking only of the miseries of his people.

But in the third month of the siege Augustine was struck down by fever. It was the approach of death.

"One day when we were all at table" (it is the Bishop Possidius who is speaking) "the saint said to us: 'You know that in this calamity I have besought God that He would deign to deliver the town of Hippo from its enemies; or if He had decided otherwise that He would deign to give His servants strength to bear the weight of His Will; or at least that He would deign to recall me to Himself.'

"As we knew the desires of the holy man, we, and all the faithful who were in the town, addressed the same prayer to God. The third month of the siege he was overcome by fever, his last sickness attacked him, and the Lord did not refuse to His servant the fruit of his prayers" (Possidius, *Augustini Vita*).

He died with admirable piety, his eyes fixed on the penitential psalms, of which he had a copy in large characters fastened to the wall of his room near his bed.

God called him to Himself, August 28th, 430, in his seventy-sixth year.

Second Book

THE DOCTRINE OF SAINT AUGUSTINE

THE doctrine of St Augustine is twofold, for he was at once a great theologian and a great philosopher. Our study would be incomplete if we failed to show him under this double aspect.

St Augustine did not indeed believe, like certain rationalists, that philosophy must necessarily deny all revealed truth as incomprehensible to reason, and that religion for the benefit of faith is obliged to banish reason. Being convinced that reason cannot contradict faith, both one and the other being the gift of God, he sought the truth for which he thirsted in the union of these two powers, instead of opposing them to each other. He says with Lacordaire: "The gospel affirms reason; and reason betrays only herself in denying the gospel. The Christian is man because of reason, the man is Christian through the gospel; thus the man and the Christian are so blended together as to form but one spirit which comes from God, the son and reflection of His indivisible light" (*Discours sur la vocation de la nation française*).

This is the doctrine of St Augustine, and this is the doctrine of the Church. For those who may be tempted to doubt it, it is sufficient to recall the following propositions, emanating from the Holy See, in which the Church claims the legitimate action of natural reason in the domain of philosophy, against the partisans of Baius, the Jansenists, and all those who affirm the impotence of human reason:

"Reasoning can prove with certainty the existence of God, the spirituality of the soul, and the free-will of man."

"Faith has followed revelation; it cannot therefore be validly invoked to prove the existence of God against atheists, or the spirituality of the soul and free-will against the partisans of naturalism and fatalism" (Decr., June 15th, 1855).

CHAPTER I

THEOLOGY OF SAINT AUGUSTINE

THE theology of St Augustine springs from the contests which he maintained victoriously against all the heresies of his day, and the numerous works which he composed to refute them. To embrace it in its full extent would overstep the limits of this work.

He opposed to the Arians the wonders accomplished by Jesus Christ, the perfection of His morality, and the fact of the human race transformed by the gospel: to the Manicheans, the indivisible unity of God and of the human soul; to the Donatists, the establishment of the Church over all the earth as the guardian of faith, the interpreter of dogma, and the dispenser of the sacraments; and to the Pelagians, the inability of the children of Adam, subject to error, and inclined to evil, to do without the Divine assistance. This last part of his doctrine is especially worthy of attention, not only because, as we are about to see, the question of grace and free-will touches the very essence of the Christian religion, but also because the difficulties which it raises have been renewed in modern times by the Calvinists, and later still by the Jansenists, who pretended to authorise their error by the doctrine of

St Augustine. Grace, on which the relations of man with God, that is to say, his whole destiny, depends, is the very foundation of Christianity, for if Jesus Christ came down to earth to ransom the human race, the coming of the Redeemer implies that human nature, fallen through original sin, could not recover its primitive innocence by its own powers, but had need of supernatural aid. On the contrary, if the intelligence is not weakened, or the will corrupted in the children of Adam, if free-will is sufficient to effect the salvation of man, grace becomes useless, and Jesus Christ sacrificed Himself in vain on Calvary. And this is what Pelagius held.

According to Pelagius the sin of Adam could recoil only on him who was the author of it.

"The propagation of the sin of Adam is incompatible with the goodness of God. Children at their birth are therefore in the same state as Adam was before his sin.

"What is called original sin is only the imitation of Adam by those who have sprung from him, and this imitation is voluntary. When St Paul says, 'All in Adam have sinned,' that simply means that all have imitated Adam in his sin; but it depended on themselves whether they followed his example; for to live without sin, it is only necessary that man should make good use of his natural faculties and his free-will.

"What is called grace is nothing else than the gift of free-will which God has made to man; and the mediation of Jesus Christ is only the example which He came to give men, as Moses gave the Law to the Israelites; this is the limit of His acts. The Law of Moses was a grace for the Jews, as the example of Jesus Christ is a grace for Christians.

"Death is not the punishment of sin; it was natural to man [1] and would have taken place all the same if Adam had not betrayed his trust. Man does not any more die by the death of Adam, than he rises by the resurrection of Jesus Christ."

We can see the artifices by which Pelagius was able for a moment to impose on the council and the Pope, to whom he had appealed from the condemnation pronounced against him. Who would not believe him orthodox when he expressly declares that he admits original sin and the necessity of grace for salvation, when he writes, "I anathematise whoever thinks or says that the assistance of God is not necessary at every moment and for every act. Let him who tries to destroy this truth be devoted to eternal punishment."

St Augustine did not allow himself to be ensnared by these equivocal protestations; he showed that Pelagius, while using the same terms as the Church, gave them an exactly opposite sense; that this assistance which God grants to human weakness was in his eyes only the gift of free-will, and the perfection of His law; in short, that by the downfall of humanity, he only understood the voluntary depravity of individuals and the bad use that they made of their liberty.

To the sophisms of Pelagius, he opposed the doctrine of the Church, founded on the Old and New Testaments.

Coming forth from the hands of God, man was in a

[1] See Appendix.

state of innocence,[1] with all his powers, corporal and spiritual, in perfect harmony, and he was not subject to death. When Adam, the father of the human race, had sinned, all his posterity bore with him the consequences of his sin, man became subject to pain, and the slave of death; his intelligence was darkened and his will weakened. Henceforth, inclined rather to evil than good, by the imperfection of his origin, he could no longer raise himself without the help of Divine grace; and this grace was given to him by the life and death of Jesus Christ, which is the gratuitous gift of the goodness and mercy of God. Grace begins and finishes the work of our salvation, enlightening our mind, and strengthening our will, exciting or predisposing it, aiding or sustaining it, co-operating with it, or perfecting it. This grace is interior; it is within us that this supernatural assistance acts; the exterior grace of the example of Jesus Christ and His doctrine could not suffice. To say with Pelagius that goodwill comes from God only, inasmuch as He has given us liberty to will good, is likewise to attribute to God a bad will, since we are able to will evil as well as good. Jesus Christ is shown to us in the gospel as the Saviour who leads us to good, not only by His example, but by communicating His righteousness to us; in the same way that Adam is pointed out to us as he who has ruined us, not by his example alone, but also by the transmission of his sin, so that as we have been made sinners by the disobedience of Adam, so

[1] See Appendix.

we are rendered righteous by the obedience of Jesus Christ. But in defending Divine grace against Pelagius, had not St Augustine sacrificed the free-will of man, without which he could not be responsible for his actions?

The reply is in the writings of St Augustine, where he ever proclaims that the will is free for good as well as evil. " Without the free-will given to the reasonable soul by God, there could be no merit for her. It is needful that man should be good, not through necessity, but freely, for he who acts through necessity, and not through free-will, does no evil " (*Contr. Fortunat.*). " God commands man not to commit adultery or other crimes; would He have imposed these commandments if man had no free-will wherewith to observe them?" (*De gratia et libero arbitr.*, iv.).

" In helping us, God does not do all our action, liberty has its part. God does not act in us as in stones, or in beings deprived of reason and will, He co-operates with us in our salvation.

" Far from denying free-will by teaching the Divine assistance, we affirm it, for even as the law is upheld by faith, so free-will is supported by Divine succour."

Notwithstanding these formal texts, which it would be easy to multiply, it has been asserted that St Augustine, while establishing gratuitous grace against Pelagius, had annihilated free-will and decided in favour of the partisans of absolute predestination. If grace is gratuitous, if it is given or refused as God pleases, are not certain men necessarily elect, and others necessarily reprobate? Such is the doctrine that Jansenius, after Calvin, pretended to find in St Augustine.

Jansenius, Bishop of Ypres, composed a book entitled "Augustinus" in which he brought together many ably grouped passages taken from St Augustine's writings, to establish, by covering himself with the authority of this great saint, a doctrine condemned by the Church, as leading to absolute predestination.

One reads in the "Augustinus": "All this shows fully and evidently that nothing is more certain and fundamental in the doctrine of St Augustine than the truth that, there are certain commandments impossible not only to the infidel, the hardened, and the blind, but also to the faithful and the just, in spite of their will and their efforts, because of their weakness; and that the grace is wanting which might render these commandments possible."

Not only St Augustine, but St Paul was put on his trial; this passage from the Epistle to the Romans, which has been so often quoted, was brought forward: "God said to Moses, I will have mercy on whom I will have mercy, and I will have pity on whom I will have pity. . . . He has mercy on whom He wills, and whom He wills He hardens." Pascal, whose good faith is above suspicion, shared this illusion when he wrote "Letters to a Provincial" in favour of the Jansenists; he thought that by admitting with St Augustine, that man can resist grace, or correspond to it when God gives it, he had protected free-will, not perceiving that by admitting that God does not give his grace to all, those to whom He refuses it are devoted to destruction according to the doctrine of the Jansenists. "They know only too well," he said, "that man by his own nature always has the power to sin and to resist grace ... but that nevertheless when it pleases God to touch him by His mercy, He makes him do what He wills and in the way He wills, without the infallibility of this operation of God in any way destroying the natural liberty of man, because of the secret and admirable manner in which God effects this change, as St Augustine has so excellently explained; which explanation scatters all the imaginary contradictions which the enemies of efficacious grace may figure to themselves between the sovereign power of grace over free-will, and the power which free-will has to resist grace. For, according to this great saint, whom the Popes of the Church have given as a rule in this matter, God changes the heart of man by the heavenly sweetness which He sheds into it; which, overcoming the delights of the flesh, causes man to feel on one side his mortality and his nothingness, and discovers to him on the other the greatness of the eternity of God, so that he conceives a disgust for the pleasures of sin which separate him from incorruptible good; and finding his greatest joy in the God who draws him, he is borne infallibly towards Him by a motion altogether free, voluntary, and amorous, so that for him it would be a trouble and a punishment to be separated from Him" (*Letter*, xviii.).

He forgot that according to Jansenius those to whom God refused this grace were destined hopelessly to destruction, and that the "Augustinus," taking but one side of St Augustine's doctrine, expressly declared "that there are certain commandments impossible, not only to the faithless, the blind, the hardened, but also to the faithful and the just, in spite of their wishes and efforts."

The Jansenists had so thoroughly identified themselves with St Augustine, and so completely attributed their doctrine to him, that when the Jesuits published an almanac which represented Jansenius with the wings of a devil, escorted by Error, Ignorance, and Fraud; the Pope, followed by Religion and the Church, hurling thunder bolts at him; and the most Christian King surrounded by Zeal, Piety and Concord, who struck at him with sceptre and sword, Port-Royal replied by a little volume in French verse, entitled: "The Illuminations of the famous Almanack of the Jesuit Fathers, entitled, The Rout and Confusion of the Jansenists, or the triumph of the Jesuit Molina over Saint Augustine."

The work began with the following lines:—

"Enfin Molina, plein de gloire
Triomphe avec sa bande noire,
Le libre arbitre audacieux
Domine la grâce des cieux;
Et l'humble Augustin en déroute
Crie, en vain, qu'au moins on l'écoute." [1]

[1] And so Molina, drunken with victory,
Triumphs with all his dark fraternity;
While man's free-will forgetful of its place
Dares plant its foot upon the neck of grace;
Put to the rout Augustine meekly flies
And vainly calls for help, while none replies.

Madame de Sévigné herself shared this illusion in spite of her faith and submission. She wrote to her daughter on the 9th June 1680: "I read books of devotion because I wish to prepare myself to receive the Holy Spirit. . . . But He breathes where it pleases Him, and He Himself prepares the hearts where He wills to dwell. It is He who prays in us with groanings that cannot be uttered[1] (Rom. viii. 26). St Augustine has said all that. I think him a good Jansenist, and St Paul also. The Jesuits have a phantom they call Jansenius which they abuse grossly; they do not seem to see how far that reaches" (*Lett.*, 817).

A phantom it certainly was not, for between the doctrine of the Church, which is that of St Paul and St Augustine, and the doctrine of Jansenius, there is an abyss. The former expressly asserts that God gives all men a *sufficing* grace, and that their goodwill can render it *efficacious*. Jansenius admits only *efficacious* grace, which God gives to some and refuses to others. According to the true doctrine, on the contrary, if some receive more and others less, for reasons unknown to us, all without exception receive enough for salvation, as shown in the beautiful parable of the Master of the Vineyard in the Gospel of St Luke, where the kingdom of Heaven is likened to the father of a household who engages some workmen for his vineyard in the morning, and hires others later in the day; but in the evening gives an equal wage to all—to those who came late as to those who came in the morning, and when the

[1] See Appendix.

latter claimed more the Master said, "Why do you complain? I do you no wrong. Did you not agree with me for a penny? Take that thine is and go thy way. I will give unto this last even as unto thee" (xv. 29).

The idea of election was the foundation of the Hebrew religion. God made for himself an elect people; but those who were not of this election were not for that reason destined to destruction, if they had desired God. That is the teaching of the gospel and the Catholic Church. God, for purposes which we cannot fathom, has elect to whom He gives peculiar graces; but He predestines none of His creatures to damnation. Such is St Paul's doctrine. There are some elect, *the children of the promise*; but none is devoted to perdition. God hardened Pharaoh's heart, but Pharaoh had rendered himself guilty. "Thou wilt say, O Israel; Those branches have been cut away that I might be grafted. That is true, they were cut off because of unbelief, and thou livest by faith. . . . They also, if they do not persevere in their unbelief, shall be grafted, for God is powerful to graft them anew" (Rom. xi. 19-22).

And this is the doctrine of St Augustine. "Sin has the power by itself to ruin all men. But the infinite mercy of God chooses from this mass of perdition elect, to whom he grants His grace and the gift of perseverance. . . . They are elect because God has freely willed to elect them and predestine them to life. There are others whom God abandons and on whom His justice is exercised. These are lost, not because they could not save themselves if they wished it, but because they find their joy and satisfaction in evil. Man can only adore the impenetrable counsels of God in His mercy as in His justice." (*De corrept.*, xiii.).

There is the City of God composed of the children of God by divine grace, and there is the City of Evil, formed of those who turn away from God. He gives Himself to the former even when they repulse him, like the Magdalen, St Paul and St Augustine. Does He refuse Himself to the others even if they seek Him? So thought Calvin and Jansenius, and so they make St Paul say, and St Augustine too, though he expressly declares the contrary.

The weighty authority of Bossuet is clear on this point:—

"Though St Augustine defended free-will so well, not only against the Manicheans, so that everyone is agreed about it, but always upheld it even against Pelagius, as shown by a hundred passages, and by entire books of his; and though he was praised by Popes, and particularly by Pope Hormisdas, for having spoken so well, not only of grace but even of free-will (*De gratia et libero arbitrio*), nevertheless, M. Simon, following the lead of Grotius, accuses him of having weakened the tradition of the Church on free-will" (Boss., *Défense de la Tradition*, X. iii.). And elsewhere: "Because of the words of Luther and Calvin, who abuse the name of St Augustine as well as St Paul, some Catholics' liking for this father has diminished. But not only has the Council of Trent taken a directly opposite view, but those who have weakly and ignorantly abandoned St Augustine, have been, so to say, punished for it immediately by the perils in which they found themselves entangled" (*Ibid.*, xxvi. 19).

Can it be said that St Augustine has resolved completely the difficult problem of the reconciliation of grace and free-will? Like those who preceded as well as those who have followed him, he established strongly the two principles without which one cannot conceive divine omnipotence or human responsibility, but he has not pretended to explain their mysterious union in a perfectly satisfying manner.

It is in the same spirit that the Church has never condemned those who, like the Molinists, give a little too much to free-will, nor those who, like the Thomists, may perhaps give a little too much to grace, provided that both one and the other recognise that free-will cannot work out salvation if grace does not come to its aid, and that grace demands the co-operation of free-will. This is what Bossuet calls "holding the two ends of the chain," and he praises St Augustine for the wise reserve he has used in these obscurities.

"How grace may be reconciled with free-will is much disputed in the schools; and perhaps even St Augustine himself has not wished to determine anything, at least fixedly—content to establish in every way the supreme sway of divine grace over the hearts of all. As to the fundamental point, which consists in allowing that God moves the will efficaciously as He pleases, all the doctors agree that this truth cannot be denied without denying the omnipotence of God, and taking away from Him the government of human affairs."

As the Pelagians, so also the Manicheans called themselves orthodox; and like them they disguised their gross heresy under specious reasoning. Nothing is more curious on this subject than the letter of Secundius, a young enthusiast of Manicheism, to Augustine, in which he considers him as a great mind gone astray since his conversion, and reproaches him with not being more Christian:

"If you had wished to make your eloquence serve truth, it would have been a great glory for us. I beg of you not to go against your nature, do not be the lance of error which pierced the side of the Saviour."

He asks himself how Augustine could leave the disciples of Manes, to join this Jewish nation, with their barbarous customs.

"Cease," he says to him, "to enclose Christ in the breast of a woman, cease to make one nature of two, for the judgment of the Lord approaches."

And he offers to enlighten Augustine in an interview which shall clear up all his doubts.

One knows what the Manicheans meant by these two natures, which they pretended to separate; they recognised, as has been said, two eternal principles; one, the principle of good, the other, the principle of evil, and when it was objected to them, that thus they destroyed the unity of God, they pretended that they were calumniated, and that their doctrine was perverted, since they admitted of and adored but one God.

St Augustine laid bare the blindness of some, and the hypocrisy of others, in his reply to Secundius, and especially in his work against the Manichean Faustus, under the form of a dialogue, which recalls the conversations of Socrates with the sophists.

Augustine.—Do you believe that there are two Gods, or that there is only one?

Faustus.—There is but one absolutely.

Augustine.—How is it then that you assert there are two?

Faustus.—We never name two Gods when we declare our faith. On what do you found these suspicions?

Augustine.—Do you not teach that there exist two principles, one of good, and the other of evil?

Faustus.—It is true that we confess two principles, but we call only one of them God. We call the other $Hyle$ or matter, or as they commonly say, the Devil. If you pretend that this is establishing two Gods, it is the same thing as affirming, that a physician who speaks of health and sickness recognises two healths (*Contra Faust.*, xxi. 4).

St Augustine had no trouble in confounding this gross sophism.

" Faustus believes he has gained his cause when he says in his defence: We do not recognise two Gods, but God and matter. But press him to say what he means by matter, and you will see that he really describes a second God. What folly to deny God as the Creator of matter, and to place the creative power in matter itself! The work of the true God you attribute to some other God, I know not whom. For whatever name you give him, it certainly is a God, it is truly another God which you impiously present to us. This is a double and a sacrilegious error, for the work of God you make to be the work of him whom you are ashamed to call God. But whatever you may do, it is a God from the moment that you confer on him the power to do what belongs to God alone.

"If the principle of evil can injure the principle of good, this last is not then immutable and incorruptible, and therefore not God. And if it is invincible, and inaccessible to any harm, how can there be an eternal struggle between it and the principle of evil? What God is this whose power is limited, lessened, and held in check by a rival principle?"

Just as they recognised two opposing principles in the world, so the Manicheans admitted two opposing souls in man, one created by the principle of good, the other by the principle of evil, struggling with each other, as did the principles of which they were the issue. As they had denied the unity of God, they denied also the unity of the soul, and with the unity of the soul, free-will and responsibility. Sin ceased to be a voluntary fault, evil was the work of the bad principle.

Augustine demonstrated victoriously, as we have seen above, that in this fatalist doctrine, which manifestly contradicted the gospel, original sin had no signification or the redemption any motive, and that the virtue of the sacraments was annihilated.

Thirdly, we find the Donatists anathematising the

Catholic Church for betraying her duty by a culpable indulgence.

There were certain Churches established whose chiefs had been declared heretical: the Donatists declared that the baptism conferred by these Churches was not valid, and that it was necessary to rebaptise those who returned to orthodoxy.

They pretended besides that there were certain faults which could not be washed away by the sacrament of penance; that, for example, there was no absolution for him who, after he had become a Christian, sacrificed again to idols to screen himself from torture, even when he repented of his weakness. St Augustine in his "Treatise on Baptism" proved that, according to the doctrine of the Church, the virtue of the sacraments is independent of the unworthiness of their administrators; that in the sacraments the sacrament itself should be considered, and not he who gives or he who receives it; that the errors of the minister, or his perverse interpretation of the words of the gospel, cannot invalidate baptism if it has been given in the name of the three Persons of the Blessed Trinity, even by heretics or schismatics. "So," the Donatists said, "you accept our baptism; then what have we less than you?" It is not your baptism we receive, replies St Augustine, it is the baptism of God and the Church. Baptism does not belong to you, what belongs to you are your perverse sentiments, your sacrilegious acts and your impious depravity. Charity is wanting to you, without which, according to the apostle's words, all is useless.

He also reproaches the Donatists with rebelling even against the command of Jesus Christ, who has given His Church power to loose, a power which applies to all sinners without distinction, provided they repent.

The Donatists say in their assemblies, " Peace be to you," and they do not wish to be at peace with the people to whom these divine words were addressed. They will not understand that one only participates in the works of sinners by approving them; and that those who, while condemning evil, do not wish to pull up the tares before the harvest lest they should root up the wheat also, have not, because of that, anything in common with sinners, but on the contrary practise the charity of our Lord, bearing for the sake of unity that which the love of righteousness makes them hate.

The Donatists, by their pride and intolerance, break the unity of the universal Church, and they separate themselves from the Saviour who has accorded mercy to the greatest sinners, and who has left His heritage to all. Notwithstanding the authority of St Cyprian, who, for a moment, was seduced by the error of the Donatists, the doctrine upheld by St Augustine has alone been declared conformable to the Christian tradition and the spirit of the Church; and the Church proclaims with him that those who separate themselves from her, but keep a certain portion of the truth, are united to her in the points of doctrine which they preserve intact; that they do not in separating from her, lose what they have carried away of her teaching; that the sanctity of the sacrament stands independent of him who, conforming to the command of Christ, administers it; and lastly, that the aim of excommunication is to lead the guilty to repentance and not to cut them off for ever from the communion of the faithful. "Love men," he writes to Petilianus, a Donatist bishop, "and slay errors. Be daring for the truth without pride, fight for the truth without violence. Pray for those whom you rebuke and for those whom you wish to persuade."

This gentleness and meekness were always practised by Augustine, even towards the most implacable adversaries.

"I beg of you all who are in the Church to take care not to insult those who are not in it. Rather ask God that they may enter. One must never constrain anyone to come back to the unity of Jesus Christ; and no arms should be employed other than discourses and reasons for fear of making false Catholics of those whom we know now as declared heretics" (*Letter* xciii.).

But later, under the influence of the excesses committed by the Donatists in Africa, Augustine admitted that Christian princes should use their authority for the triumph of the faith, yet with moderation towards the rebels. "I have yielded to the instances which my colleagues have opposed to my arguments, for my first feeling was not to force anyone to Christian unity, but to act by words, to fight by discussion, and to conquer by reason. It is not argument but experience which has modified my opinion" (*Ibid.*).

This grave question was raised again in the seventeenth century, at the time of revocation of the Edict of Nantes, and those who favoured measures of repression did not fail to recall the Donatists and St Augustine.

We read in a memoir of M. de Lamoignon de Basville, Lieutenant of the province of Languedoc, entitled: "Doubts about the newly-converted, proposed to the Bishop of Meaux."

"The question is, whether the newly-converted should be forced to the duties of religion, and to go to mass. Is not this question decided clearly by St Augustine? He was first of opinion that no constraint should be used, but he came round to a contrary opinion. Can one believe that he changed his ideas without having gone deeply into the matter? He hints the reason of his hesitation when he says: *Ne fictos catholicos haberemus quos apertos hæreticos noveramus* (*Ep.* cxviii. *ad Vincent*), *i.e.*, for fear of making false Catholics of those whom we know as declared heretics.

"But, moreover, this is the opinion not only of St Augustine, it is also that of a great number of bishops who obliged him to change, by bringing before him such convincing reasons that he was forced to give in to them; and the strongest reasons were the dispositions of the Donatists themselves, who were held back by the prejudices of their birth, by false shame, and by other motives, which are so well explained in St Augustine's letter to Vincentius. It is what he calls *demonstrantium exempla* (*Ep.* cxiii.).

"One may say that this situation of the Donatists is

the true portrait of their state, who now find themselves among the newly-converted; they feel the same weaknesses, they are kept back by the same prejudices, they for the most part demand the same assistance to enable them to follow in the path they have chosen. If it is to be feared that their dissimulation may profane our mysteries, would not St Augustine have employed this argument, supposing that it had struck him? He does not, however, say a word of it, and if the bishops of that age had had this scruple, would not Vincentius as a Donatist bishop have raised it, and used it as his strongest argument to combat St Augustine? He replied to all his other objections, but he did not mention this; must one not conclude, therefore, that they did not then make the same difficulty, and that the general good of religion overbore these private considerations? If it was a wound, it was, he said, useful to the Church in the same way as an incision is to a tree on which a branch is grafted which will one day bear good fruit."

And after having invoked the authority of the fathers of the Church, the Councils, the Sovereign Pontiffs, and the edicts of the emperors, he adds with an evident desire of moderation: "Instead of saying that the mysteries are profaned, would it not be more expedient to conclude that the Church is always content, without making any kind of inquisition, to instruct those who are present, when the converts have been received by a solemn abjuration to tolerate them in hopes of a sincere conversion; and especially when the Catholic Church has been in the ascendant so that irreverence need not be feared by reason of the people's obedience and submission to the orders of the magistrate; when favourable inclinations have been observed in the persons converted, and when a great number need only to be determined by some kind of constraint sufficient to break through the ties which kept them back. If at times there has been a contrary usage, it has been when the Catholic Church was not at her strongest, when scandal was to be feared, when there was no well-founded hope of true conversion, or, finally, when the mysteries of our faith were not manifested and held in as great veneration as they are now."

And seeing that the greater number consists of "those who are much shaken, who would wish to have taken the better part, and who still have some difficulty in declaring themselves," he inclines seemingly to the first opinion of St Augustine: "Will you leave this great number of persons to perish, who have good intentions, and who may be condemned because of the incredulity of others? And may we not apply here St Augustine's maxim which he laid down in a similar case for the treatment of the Donatists, that it is an inevitable necessity to tolerate in the Church the good and the bad." One sees by the reply of Bossuet that he leans towards the second opinion of St Augustine. "If no constraint is brought to bear on them I am convinced that all is lost."

It is the same with the bishop of Montauban, who inclines towards the measures taken against the

Donatists, measures which St Augustine ended by approving.

"The whole difficulty is then to know if the newly-converted should be obliged to go to mass. It seems that one cannot do better here than follow the maxims and the conduct which the Church in Africa used with regard to the Donatists. We know that it was a very learned Church, filled with the Spirit of God, especially in the time of St Augustine, and very exact in Catholic discipline. Everyone knows what the schism of the Donatists was in its origin and its progress; it is sufficient to remark that the Donatists were very powerful in Africa, that they had towns, provinces, churches, and bishops; that they erected altar against altar; and that the schism became so considerable, that it was not yet extinct in the sixth century, as one sees in the letters of Pope St Gregory.

"The Catholic bishops neglected neither exhortations, prayers, nor amiable and pacific conferences to bring the Donatists back. Several who had been put in the places of schismatic prelates deprived of their sees offered to give them up if they would renounce their errors and return to unity. But the ways of peace were all useless, and the Church in Africa was at last constrained to have recourse to the secular powers and the authority of the emperors. . . . The effect of the declarations of the emperor, of which the principle was charity, was so great, that nearly all Africa was converted. . . .

"It was this crowd of sudden conversions which made St Augustine change his sentiments. He had believed at first, against the counsel of the ancient bishops of Africa, that the Donatists should not be constrained, and that one should regard instruction as the only lawful means to be used, and that long-suffering and patience towards them were the rules of Christian charity. These reasons, which are indeed specious, impressed him for a long time, but when he saw the town of Thagaste, where he was born, and a great part of Africa reunited by the fear of punishment to the Catholic Church, he gave in to the common opinion of his colleagues. Experience strengthened his opinion so much on this subject that he composed two letters on it to Vincent and Count Boniface, which the present controversy has rendered celebrated."

One sees that if St Augustine ended through the force of circumstances by admitting constraint, he was, as has been shown above, naturally drawn to gentleness and mildness.

Let us add the witness of P. Lacordaire to the rest.

"All Christians were convinced that faith was a free act, of which grace was the only source. All said with St Athanasius, 'The characteristic of a religion of love is to persuade not to compel'" (*Epist. ad Erem.*). But they were not agreed on the degree of liberty which should be accorded to error. This second question appeared to them quite different from the first, for it is one thing not to do violence to consciences, and quite another thing to abandon them to the arbitrary action of an evil intellectual force. Those who wished for absolute liberty spoke thus by the mouth of St Hilary, Bishop of Poitiers. " Let it be permitted to us to deplore the misery of our age and the crazy opinions of a day in which it is believed that God can be protected by man and the Church of Jesus Christ by the power of the world. I ask you, O Bishops, on what succours did the apostles rely for preaching the gospel? What sort of men did they call to their assistance in preaching Jesus Christ? How did they convert the nations from the worship of idols to that of the true God? Did those who, on receiving stripes and chains, praised God, get their dignity from the palace? Was it with the edicts of a prince that Paul, exposed as a criminal, assembled the Church of Christ? Or was it indeed under the patronage of Nero, Vespasian, Decius, or of any of those whose hatred but made the Divine Word to blossom? Those who lived by the labour of their hands, who held secret assemblies, who wandered over villages, towns, and nations, by land and by sea, despite decrees of the senate, or edicts of princes, had they not the keys of the kingdom of Heaven? And has not Christ been the more preached, according as it has been forbidden to preach Him? But now, O sorrow! the suffrages of the world serve as a recommendation to divine faith, and Christ is convicted of weakness by the very intrigues made on His behalf! That same Church now spreads terror by exile and prison, and compels men to believe in her who of old was believed in because she endured exile and prison; and she who has been consecrated by the hand of persecutors now depends on the condescension of those who communicate with her" (*Contra Auxentium*).

St Augustine who at first belonged to this school, addressed the Manicheans in the same spirit: "Let those be severe with you who do not know with what labour truth is discovered, and how hardly one escapes error. Let those treat you rigorously who do not know how rare and difficult it is to vanquish the phantoms of sense by the serenity of a saintly intelligence. Let those treat you rigorously who do not know with what difficulty and trouble the inward eye of man is healed, so that he shall be rendered capable of seeing his Sun, not this sun which you worship, and which shines before the fleshly eyes of man and beast, but He of whom the prophet writes: *The Sun of righteousness hath arisen for me;* and of whom the Gospel says that *He is the light that lighteth every man that cometh into the world.* Those may treat you with rigour who do not know with what sighs and groans one comes to understand God even ever so little. In short, those may treat you with severity who have never been deceived by the error which deceives you" (*Contra Epist. Manich.*).

St Augustine passed later to the opposite school, on account of the fury of the Donatists in Africa against the Church. He thought that he owed this to the experience of two truths which meditation on the gospel had not taught him: one, that error is essentially persecuting, and never grants truth the least possible liberty; the other, that there is an oppression of weak minds by strong minds, in

THEOLOGY OF SAINT AUGUSTINE 109

the same way as there is an oppression of feeble bodies by robust bodies. From which he concluded that the repression of error is a legitimate defence against two tyrannies—the tyranny of persecution and the tyranny of seduction.

I am nothing more than an historian in this matter. Nevertheless this second school was worked on like the first, though in a less degree, by the inevitable necessity of Christian gentleness, and St Augustine wrote to Donatus· pro-consul of Africa (*Letter*, cxxvii.), these very remarkable words on the subject of the most aggressive heretics who ever lived: "We wish that they may be corrected, but not put to death, that a disciplinary repression may be exercised with regard to them, but that they may not be given up to the punishments which they have deserved. If you take away the lives of these men for their crimes, you will prevent like causes being brought before your tribunal, and then the boldness of our enemies rising to its zenith will finish our ruin, by the necessity in which you will have put us of preferring to die by their hands rather than accuse them before your judgment seat" (Lacordaire, *Memoires pour le rétablissement des Frères Prêcheurs*, ch. iv.).

Augustine showed the same moderation in the celebrated discussion which he had with Jerome on the interpretation of a passage from the gospel. About 395 Augustine, then a simple priest at Hippo, had written to Jerome to express his admiration, and to submit his works to him, asking him to examine and judge them with severity. At the same time, he respectfully expressed his doubts on the explanation which Jerome had given of the following passage of St Paul's Epistle to the Galatians:

"When Cephas (St Peter) came to Antioch I withstood him openly, because he was worthy of reproach. For indeed before the coming of certain persons from James he ate with the Gentiles; but when they came, he drew back and kept himself apart from the Gentiles, fearing those who were circumcised. And the other Jews used the same dissimulation, so that Barnabas himself was led away by them. But when I saw that they walked not aright according to the truth of the gospel, I said to Cephas in presence of them all: If thou who art a Jew livest as the Gentiles and not as the Jews, how dost thou constrain the Gentiles to observe the customs of the Jews?" (Gal. ii. 11-14).

Jerome, in commenting on these words of St Paul's, thought that he had only pretended to blame St Peter, for deferring to the opinion of those who might have been wounded by his conduct, and that one ought only to see a sort of "official simulation" in these reproaches which were addressed to him. Augustine represented to Jerome the danger of an interpretation which introduced lying[1] into the Holy Books; he reminded him that St Paul, considering the ceremonies of the Jewish law as imperfect figures of the New Law, could not have thought that they ought to bind the Gentiles by it, and therefore he did right in resisting St Peter when the latter obliged the Gentiles to

[1] See Appendix.

pass through the Mosaic observances before becoming Christians. Augustine modestly drew the attention of the learned doctor of Bethlehem to this point, but unfortunately the letter never arrived at its destination, and when Augustine became a bishop he wrote a second on the same subject. Copies of this were circulated in Italy before it reached Jerome, and they persuaded him that the Bishop of Hippo had composed a work against him. Jerome was wounded by this; he did not, however, reply till 402, and then he refused, not without some bitterness, to enter into discussion with Augustine, alleging his great age as an excuse, abstaining, he said, from judging the works of a bishop of his communion, and contenting himself with criticising his own without touching those of others. He ended by begging him to make sure whenever he wrote to him in future that he had received his former letters. As to the heart of the question, he limited himself to stating that his opinion was that of Origen and of the Greek doctors, and he was content, he said, to follow the opinion of the elders.

Augustine reproached himself with having offended the old man, he humbled himself to him, and spared nothing to appease him.

"There is not, and there never can be, in me as much knowledge of the Divine Scriptures as I know there is in you, and the small share of this knowledge which I have acquired I dispense to God's people, as my ecclesiastical business hinders me from giving myself up to this study, beyond the needs of the people whom I am bound to instruct."

But for all that he did not give up what he believed to be the truth; he remained persuaded that the reproach of St Paul could not have been simulated when he said to St Peter that he was not walking according to the truth of the gospel when he let the Gentiles believe that Jewish ceremonies were necessary before coming to Jesus Christ.

Jerome did not give in immediately. After a long and subtle discussion, he concluded that Augustine's opinion and his own differed very little one from the other. "After all," he wrote, "there is not a great difference between your opinion and mine. I say that Peter and Paul for fear of the Jews pretended to fulfil the precepts of the law. You hold that they did it out of charity, not by dissimulation but by affectionate compassion. Therefore, whether through fear or mercy, it remains established that the two apostles pretended to be what they were not." This was eluding the question and diminishing its importance. St Paul had reproached St Peter with allowing it to be believed, contrary to the gospel, that it was necessary to fulfil the observances of the Jewish law, and this had been an obstacle to the establishment of the Christian Faith. This is why Augustine held that there was a reason for the reproach, although he recognised that the apostles had been obliged to *tolerate* the Mosaic ceremonies for some time, so as to allow them to fall away by degrees, and as he says *to bury the synagogue honourably*; and again in this, without possessing Jerome's vast erudition, Augustine showed himself the clear-sighted interpreter of Christian thought. He understood the great importance of the discussion which Jerome strove to diminish, for to exact that everyone should become a Jew before becoming a Christian, was to make the conversion of the heathen almost impossible, not only by imposing on them practices likely to repel them, but also in obliging them to become Jews, that is to say, that they should abandon their nationality to take another which they considered inferior.

M. Renan, the author of the *Vie de Jesus* and of *Saint Paul*, is not deceived (and his is not evidence to be suspected) as to the gravity of the point in dispute, and the wisdom with which it was decided: "When they came to circumcision, and the obligation of fulfilling the law, the difference of opinion burst out in all its force. The Pharisian party upheld its pretentions in the most absolute manner. The party of emancipation replied with triumphant vigour. It cited several cases where the uncircumcised had received the Holy Ghost, and if God made no distinction between heathen and Jews, how should any man have the audacity to make one for Him? How could they hold for defiled what God had purified? Why impose on the neophytes a yoke which the race of Israel had not been able to bear? It is by Jesus that we are saved, and not by the law. . . . The most admirable trait in the history of the origin of Christianity is, that this profound and radical division, bearing on a point of the first importance, did not cause in the Church a complete schism which would have been its ruin. . . . A superior bond—the love that all had for Jesus, the remembrance by which all lived, was stronger than the divisions. The most fundamental dissension which was ever produced in the bosom of the Church did not lead to an anathema. . . . The conversion of the Gentiles was admitted as legitimate. . . . All gave their consent openly to Paul and Barnabas, and admitted their divine right to the apostolate of the pagan world."

Jerome finished by recognising that the truth was on the side of his opponent. We have proof of it in a letter of Augustine to one of his friends, in which he quotes a significant passage from the *Critobulus* of Jerome, a work designed to refute the Pelagians, and in which Jerome declares that it is very difficult to find even bishops absolutely blameless, " since St Paul found occasion to reprove even St Peter" (S. Aug., *Letter*, clx.).

CHAPTER II

PHILOSOPHY OF SAINT AUGUSTINE

REASON precedes faith, for it is she who judges that the authority which teaches revealed truths to us is worthy of our belief. Credulity is blind, but the faith which the Catholic Church demands rests upon proofs furnished by reason.

If one did not first believe in God, how could one believe in the word of God? Belief in revealed truths presupposes belief in truth known by the light of reason alone. One reads in the *Pensées* of Pascal: "Reason would never submit did she not judge that there are occasions when she ought to submit." These are nearly the words of St Augustine in a letter addressed to Consentius.

But reason's part does not end here; it continues after the acceptance of faith. Among the truths which faith teaches us there are some beyond the range of our reason, and others which are accessible to it. Not to seek to convince ourselves of these last by reason, would be to renounce the legitimate exercise of a faculty which God has implanted in us, which raises us above the animals, and co-operates in our knowledge of the truth (*De utilit. cred.*, vii.).

Faith comes to the assistance of this faculty, teaches the truths which it cannot attain to, confirms those which are in its domain, instructs the feeble-minded, represses the rashness of those who believe only in reason, but undeceives those who, refusing to believe in it, declare it powerless to give certainty (*De utilit. cred.*, x.).

Those who pretend that human reason is incapable of arriving at truth, and that all our knowledge is uncertain, refute themselves by the contradiction into which they necessarily fall.

The new academicians tell us that we cannot attain truth, and that we must hold to what seems true. But to say that a thing seems true, is it not to affirm that it resembles truth? and how can we judge that it resembles truth if we do not know truth itself? "If someone on seeing your brother asserts that he resembles your father whom he has never seen, would he not appear to you absurd?" (*Contr. acad.*, ii. 8).

"I do not fear the arguments of the academicians against the truths which I set forth. If you deceive yourself? they say. But if I deceive myself, I exist; that which does not exist cannot deceive itself; therefore I do exist if I deceive myself" (*City of God*, xi. 26).

"Whoever knows that he doubts something, knows something true, for since he knows that he has this doubt he knows with certainty something true. Thus he who doubts if he has a truth, has in him a truth of which he does not doubt "(*De vera relig.*, xxxix).

It is in reality the *Cogito, ergo sum* of Descartes, on which all the Cartesian system rests: I doubt, then I think; I think, then I am.

Pascal seems to believe that St Augustine did not know the full bearing of this. "I am far from saying that Descartes may not be the real author of it even if he should have learnt it in the reading of this great saint, for I know what a difference there is between writing a sentence by chance, without any further sort of reflection upon it, and perceiving in this sentence an admirable chain of consequences which proves the difference between the material and spiritual nature" (Pascal, *Espr. géom. et raison*, ii.).

Descartes expressed the same idea in a letter which it is supposed was addressed to M. de Zuytlichem, Nov. 11th, 1640: "I am obliged to you for bringing the passage of St Augustine to my notice which bears some relation to my *I think, therefore I am*; I went to the library in this town to-day to read it, and I find that he really uses it to prove the certainty of our existence, and afterwards to show that there is in us a reflection of the Trinity; in the fact that we are; and that we know we are; and that we love this being and this knowledge which is in us; whereas I use it to make known that this "I" which thinks, is an immaterial substance with nothing corporeal about it. But these are two very different things. I am none the less pleased at having met with St Augustine were it only for the sake of shutting the mouth of the little minds who have tried to cry out against this principle."

Pascal and Descartes are wrong. It is not with St Augustine a passing glimpse of a truth. He incessantly comes back to it, and he reproduces in various forms in a great number of works this argument which invincibly ruins scepticism.[1]

First, in the "Treatise on the Trinity" where he expresses himself thus: "If one doubts, it is because one lives, it is because one seeks to assure oneself; if one doubts one thinks; if one doubts, it is that one knows one does not know; if one doubts, it is because one judges that one should not believe lightly; even he who doubts of all the rest cannot doubt of these things, for without these things, to doubt would be impossible" (*De Trinit.*, x.).

Afterwards, in the book of the "Soliloquies," he imagines a dialogue between reason and himself.

"*Reason.*—Do you know what you want?

"*Augustine.*—I do not.

"*Reason.*—Do you know what you think?

"*Augustine.*—I do." (*Soliloq.*, ii. 1.)

And as Descartes did later, it is by thought that St Augustine proves that the soul is spiritual, for knowing that she thinks and knowing it without the intervention of the organs of sense, and without the help of the body, she is, and she can only be, what she knows of herself, that is to say, thought and not matter.

In all this part of his doctrine, which agrees both with Cartesian and Christian "spiritualism," St Augustine breathes of the platonic philosophy which had inclined him towards Christianity.

Not only does he declare with Plato that the soul is truly distinct from matter, and that it must be set free from the body and disengaged from the senses

[1] See Appendix.

to seize on the highest truths (*De Genes. ad lit.*, vii. 14), but he further proclaims that the light which enlightens the soul is altogether interior and does not come from without. Plato says, "When the eyes turn towards objects which are not illuminated by the sun, they can hardly discern them, and seem attacked by blindness, as if they had lost the power of seeing. But when they look at the things lit up by the sun, they see them distinctly. The same thing occurs with regard to the soul. When she gazes on what is lit up by truth and by being, she understands, she knows, she shows that she is gifted with intelligence. But when she turns her eyes on what is mingled with obscurity, on that which is born and dies, her gaze becomes troubled and darkened, she has no longer anything but uncertain opinions, and she hovers between one and the other" (Plato, Rep., vi.).

Let us hear St Augustine: "We see the sun with our bodily eyes; it is with the mind's eye that each man perceives that he lives, that he wills, that he seeks, that he knows or does not know. In reading this you will recall having seen the sun with the eyes of the body, you can even see at the same moment that he is on the horizon. But to see that which is revealed to the mind, that is to say, that you live, that you wish to know God, that you seek to know Him, that you know that you live, that you wish what you seek for, that you are ignorant how one can know God, you do not use your bodily eyes and you have no need of choosing a place to gaze on these things.

... It is therefore in yourself that you see them, and that you apprehend them, without any figure or any colour. And they appear to you with all the more clearness and certainty, as you contemplate them with a more interior gaze." (*Letter* cxlvii.)

But St Augustine does not go so far as to conclude with Plato, that because the soul has often to sustain a struggle against the body, there is therefore between soul and body an absolute incompatibility, that the soul is in the body as in a prison, that it can only know truth by separating itself in some sort from the body, in short that it can only attain its perfection by securing a divorce from the body.

"Is there anything more difficult," says Plato (*Phaedo*), "than to think with thought alone, disengaged from every outside and sensible element, to apply directly the pure essence of thought in oneself, to the search of the essence of each thing in itself, without the ministration of the eyes and the ears, or any intervention of the body, which only troubles the soul and hinders it in finding the knowledge of the truth, however little commerce she may have with it? .... As long as we have our body, and that our soul is bound to this evil element, we shall never possess the object of our desires—that is to say, truth."

St Augustine doubtless was not ignorant (for who could know better than he?) of this warfare of spirit against flesh, which St Paul has expressed so strongly in his Epistle to the Romans (ch. vii.): "I perceive another law in my members which struggles against the law of reason, and renders me captive to the law of sin that is in my members." But if he attests the fact of these internal conflicts, of which he has had sad experience, if he believes in the necessity of purifying the soul by the conquest of the senses, his reason affirms that the body, which Plato considered but the prison of the soul, is the instrument appropriate to its needs, its helper and its servant, sometimes rebellious but more often docile; and the Christian doctrine of the resurrection of the body confirms him in his opinion, since from it follows that, the body is essential to the fuller life of the soul albeit the bodies of the elect will be "glorified," that is to say, exempt from the gross necessities of earthly life. St Augustine reproaches Plato with having admitted that the soul has existed without the body, and before the body in an anterior life, that it will finally exist without the body, that it can pass from one body to another, and in a word, that it is the nature of the soul to live apart, and that it is a punishment for it to be united to the body (*City of God*, x. 31, and *Retract.*, i. 8). He affirms, on the contrary, that it is not the essence of either of these substances to live without the other, that their union is the work of God, that each without the other is unformed and incomplete[1] (*Confess.*, xiii. 2, and xii. 3), and that we can no more conceive of the soul without its body, than the heathen could conceive of Jupiter without his thunder-bolt. "We must not, then, when we sin accuse the flesh in itself and throw back this reproach on the Creator, since the flesh is

[1] See Appendix.

good of its kind" (*City of God*, xiv. 5). "Let the Platonists, then, cease to threaten us with the body as with a punishment, and let them not propose for our adoration a divinity whose work they exhort us to fly from and reject."

We have indeed seen with the ancients as with the moderns into what aberrations and mistakes certain mystics have fallen, by admitting and driving to its extreme deduction this doctrine of Plato, on the absolute divorce of soul and body, of the spiritual and material substances; and how the soul, by despising the body, "this rag" comes at last, no longer to watch over the animal inclinations, so as not to sink from its dignity or to distract itself from its high aims; and thus it leaves the body to act according to its pleasure, while the soul inhabits ideal regions.

St Augustine, guided by his strong good sense, had divined on this point the doctrine of St Thomas Aquinas. In fact, this great doctor, correcting Plato by Aristotle, decided on the relations of soul and body in the same way as St Augustine. Like him, he combated this excess of the platonic doctrine, and declared that the alliance of body and soul, far from being a union against nature, is ordained by God; that what the Greek philosopher considered as a discord, is a true concord; that if the body ought to be subordinate to the soul as being its inferior, the two substances are none the less associated in a common work, co-operating to the same end, and that were it otherwise, one could not explain how, from the birth of the child, body and soul keep up without effort such constant relations as generally attest a perfect agreement and a complete harmony. "St Augustine," says St Thomas (*Quæst.*, lxxv., *art.* 4), "praises Varro for having said that man is neither soul alone, nor body alone, but body and soul united." And he sums up his opinion in this formula: "The soul cannot arrive at its perfection without the body," a formula which is diametrically opposed to that of Plato (*Quæst., disput., q.* iii., *art.* 10; *cf. Quæst.*, lxxv., *art.* 4).

For Plato the ideal of the perfection of the soul is not the domination of the soul over the body, but the absolute rupture of the soul with the body, considered not as its auxiliary and its instrument, but as its irreconcilable enemy.

If in later times Malebranche and Fénélon inclined, not without danger, towards the platonic mysticism, Bossuet, on the contrary, pronounced for the Thomist and Augustinian doctrine: "The body," says Bossuet (*Connaissance de Dieu et de soi-même*, iii. 20), " is therefore not a simple instrument applied from outside, nor a ship which the soul, as pilot, governs; it would be thus with her if she were simply intellectual; but because she is sensitive, she is forced to interest herself in the most intimate way with what touches her, and to govern it not as a strange object, but as something naturally and intimately united to her. In a word, the soul and body make together but one natural whole, and there is between the parts a perfect and necessary communication."

St Augustine returned to platonism when the question arose of fixing the source of truth.

We have seen that as the bodily eyes can perceive nothing if they have not the sunlight during the day, in the same way an interior light is necessary to illumine reason, which is the eye of the soul; and this inward light enlightens minds, as the sun enlightens the eyes, and it is with this light that souls see all truth. With Plato, Augustine conceives this truth as residing eternally in the *Logos*, which emanates from God, and which he identifies with the Eternal "Word." He declares in the "Confessions," as we have already seen, that he did not understand the Gospel of St John till he had studied the books of the Platonists: "And therein I read, not indeed in the very words, but to the very same purpose, enforced by many and divers reasons, that *In the beginning was the Word, and the Word was with God, and the Word was God: the same was in the beginning with God: all things were made by Him and without Him was nothing made: that which was made in Him was life, and the life was the light of men, and the light shineth in the darkness, and the darkness comprehended it not:*[1] and that the soul of man, though it *bears witness to the light*, yet itself *is not that light;* but the Word of God, being God, *is that true light that lighteth every man that cometh into the world*[2] (*Confess.*, vii. 9). Thus for Augustine, as for Plato, the truth which man finds in himself is none other thing than the truth of God; in God it dwells from all eternity. "It is immutable because it comprehends all things immutably created, and because you cannot say such a truth belongs to you rather than to me or to

[1] John i. 1-5.   [2] *Ib.* 9.

another; and because it gives itself universally to all; and because it is not susceptible of change, as is our spirit which receives it; and because it is not limited as the soul is, or increased when I see more and diminished when I see less; but remains unalterable and always pure. And when we read something true, it is neither the book nor the author of the book which makes us find it true, but something superior which enlightens us, and which is the truth of God " (*Lett.*, xix.).

This doctrine was identified for St Augustine with the theory of *Ideas*, which is the foundation of Plato's philosophy. One knows that Plato distinguishes the *sensible* realities which compose this changing and imperfect world from the *intelligible* realities or *Ideas*, that is to say Ideals, the eternal and perfect patterns of the sensible realities which are united in God, who is the Idea of Good, the supreme Ideal. The Ideas are, therefore, the immutable and invisible types of changing and visible things, the eternal realities whose shadows alone we perceive here below.

Philosophy delivers man from the bonds which fetter him to these shadows, and raises him from the world of sense to the world of intelligence, where he contemplates pure Ideas. But reason does not raise itself immediately to this contemplation of the Idea of Good, which is the height of knowledge. To attain this it passes through an intermediate degree, which is the knowledge of abstract truths, and of mathematical deductions; for Plato considered numbers and mathematical laws as the realisation of laws of human understanding in matter, as a certain harmony, and order, imprinted in our nature by the eternal geometrician.

St Augustine wished that reason should follow this ascending march, whose steps he had successively climbed himself. "And thus by degrees I passed from bodies to the soul, which through the bodily senses perceives; and thence to its inward faculty, to which the bodily senses represent things external, whitherto reach the faculties of beasts; and thence again to the reasoning faculty, to which what is received from the senses of the body is referred to be judged. Which finding itself also to be in me a thing variable made a last effort to rise to a conception of something still higher and drew away my thought from all customary illusions, and from the phantoms of the imagination which had so long beset it, that so it might find what that light was whereby reason itself was enlightened; until at last, all doubting ended, it cried out, 'That the unchangeable was to be preferred to the changeable'" (*Confess.*, vii. 17).

Like Plato, he demands that the soul before springing towards this supreme region, should be tested by the culture of the sciences; like him also, he recognises between the world of appearances and the world of realities an intermediate region, which is the object of mathematical sciences and the principle of the harmony of things.

"This harmony, which does not reside in a constant and certain manner in sensible numbers, but whose image and fugitive appearance we find here below, how should it be desired by the soul if its ideal existed nowhere? Now it is not found in any point of space or of time; space is unequal, and time passing. Where shall we place it? Reply if thou canst. It is not in the forms of the body; it does not belong to the eyes to determine its exact proportion. It is not in the divisions of time. We know not if they are longer or shorter than they ought to be. Where then does this harmony reside which we long to find in form and in the movement of bodies, and for which we cannot trust to them? It is only found in what is superior to the body, in the soul, and in what is superior to the soul."

Visible creatures are, therefore, the degrees by which we are raised little by little to their invisible author. But although the wonders of creation tell of their author it is not with the eyes of the body that we seek God; we can only see Him and know Him with the eyes of the soul, which is made in His image. For St Augustine, then, as for all great spiritual philosophers, the real proof of the existence of God and His infinite perfection is the absolute truths which are the foundation of human reason, and which passing beyond its range cannot be its work, but must exist eternally in an absolute and eternal Being.

"If you find nothing above our reason but what is eternal and immutable, will you hesitate to call such a being God? Now you are forced to recognise that the body and the reason are subject to change. If then without any intervention of the body and by itself reason perceives something eternal and immutable, does it not necessarily recognise its God, and avow at the same time that it is dependent on Him ?"

Pascal says, and rightly, that these metaphorical proofs of the existence of God do not act on the soul, but on the reason alone: " If a man should be persuaded that the proportions of numbers are immaterial truths, eternal and dependent on first truth in which they exist and whom they call God, I do not think that he is much advanced towards his salvation" (Pascal, *Pensées*, x. 5).

St Augustine admits this as well as Pascal, but he does not disdain to appeal to reason in battling against atheists as he had done in refuting sceptics. And Bossuet in his philosophical treatise, *De la Connaissance de Dieu et de soi-même*, does not seek any other proof of the existence of God than the same that St Augustine has drawn from the necessary truths: "All these truths exist independently of all time. Eternal and immutable as they are, if I seek where or in what subject they exist, I am obliged to confess a Being in whom truth is eternally existent, and from whom is derived the truth that may be in anything which is, and understood to be, outside of Him. . . . This eternal object is God, eternally existent, eternally the truth, eternally pure. . . . Necessarily, therefore, there is something which is, before all time, from all eternity, and it is in this Eternal that these eternal truths exist. It is also there that I see them" (Bossuet, *Conn. de Dieu*, iv. 5).

These same absolute and eternal truths are the

foundation of the moral law. St Augustine finds in them the rule of our conduct, as well as the rule of our judgments. " The moral law is nothing else than the sovereign reason imprinted on us, and according to which it is right that all should be in order. This law is universal, and immutable, it escapes from all vicissitudes, all men know it as they know God. It is anterior to the law of Moses and suffices to condemn those who do evil, and at the same time that it shows itself to reason it is felt by the heart. Like the evangelic law, this natural law is written in all consciences, it bids man live according to justice, to draw away his heart from the goods which perish, to turn it to the eternal riches, it bids him subject his body to his soul and purify his soul so as it may approach God. He who observes the moral law, and respects justice only through fear of punishmeut, is not truly just. He would do evil if he were not afraid of being punished. One must love justice and abstain from evil, through love of good " (*Lett.*, clvii.).

" To love good, is to love God; and the love of God includes the love of one's neighbour." " Perfect virtue is the love of what should be loved " (*Lett.*, clv.).

This conception of the moral law is equally that of Bossuet. " It is by this superior light that we see if we have done well or ill. . . . It is there that we see with all other truths the invariable rules for our conduct " (Bossuet *Conn. de Dieu*, iv. 5).

Divine reason, which is the eternal and primordial exemplar of all beings, is at the same time the sovereign law which rules them, a necessary law when it directs beings deprived of reason and liberty; simply obligatory, when it would govern free and reasonable beings. Enlightened by eternal truth reason serves as a guide to the will, but the will can refuse to follow this guide. The will is a movement of the soul which of itself and without anything forcing it, leads us to repulse or to seek an object. It is to the attraction of things that the will yields, carried towards what pleases it, turned from what displeases it, solicited by divers and often opposing allurements, and ready to follow that which is most vivid, if choice does not intervene as the moderating power of the will. At the moment when it is divided between the attraction of moral good, and the attraction of passion, the will suspends its determination to give reason time to enlighten it in its choice, to show it passion unveiled and despoiled of its passing seductiveness, and duty with its durable beauty. If the attraction of duty conquers, choice, confirming its victory, sets the will in motion towards good. If the attraction of passion is the stronger, choice accepts the defeat and allows the will to turn towards evil.

Choice in man is therefore the force which gives its consent to good or evil; it was given to man that he might live according to order. And when God punishes the sinner it is as if He said: "Why dost thou not use thy choice to live well, since I gave it to thee for that purpose" (*De spirit. et litt.*, xxxi., xxxiii.).

Certain men to escape the responsibility of their acts, invoke the divine prescience. God possesses omniscience: He knows, and He embraces with a look, the past, the present, and the future. If he knows in advance what I shall do, my act is arrested, and fixed by every necessity. I cannot act otherwise, therefore I am no longer free or responsible.

"We are in no wise reduced to the alternative of denying choice, or free-will, to save the foreknowledge of God, or of denying the foreknowledge of God—by a sacrilege, to save free-will. But we embrace these two principles, and we confess both one and the other with the same faith and the same sincerity: the foreknowledge, in order to believe well, and the free-will, in order to live well. How indeed could we possibly live well without believing of God what we ought to believe of Him? Let us beware then of denying the prescience of God, under the pretext of wishing to be free, since it is God whose grace gives us liberty.

"No, it is not in vain that there are laws, that one has recourse to reproofs, to exhortations, to blame, to praise; for God has foreseen all these things, and they have precisely the effect which He foresaw they would have, in the same way that prayer serves to obtain from Him those blessings which He has foreseen He would grant to those who pray to Him.

"There is therefore justice in rewarding the good and in punishing the wicked, a man does not sin because God has foreseen that he would sin; on the contrary, it is beyond all doubt that when he sins, it is he that sins, He whose prescience is infallible having foreseen that his sin, far from being the effect of his fate or fortune, had no other cause than his own will. It is also without doubt that if he does not wish to sin he will not sin; but then God will have foreseen that he will not wish to sin" (*City of God*, v. 10).

But how is it that God permits evil, suffering, sin? Why has He made man fallible? If His creature is bad is not God who has created him the author of evil? As Boethius said in his prison: "Whence does evil come if God exists? And if He does not exist, whence comes Good?" St Augustine's reply is that which Leibnitz developed later in his theodicy. God not being able to give to his creatures infallibility—that is, the sinlessness which belongs to the perfect being,—every creature is necessarily limited, and imperfect; it is in fact the very condition of its being,—"metaphysical evil," as they call it in the schools. Physical evil or suffering is but the condition for receiving supreme good; it is a passing trial to be followed by endless happiness. It teaches us to value lightly earthly joys and sorrows which are common to the wicked and the good, so as to attach us to the true happiness which belongs to the good only. When we come to the supreme judgment of God, we shall recognise the excellence of his justice.

As to moral evil, that is to say sin, God could not free man from it except by depriving him of a real good, and by making him like the brute a slave to instinct, knowing neither good or evil. He created man free that he might love and practise good, and thereby merit and obtain happiness. Moral evil, which is the only real evil, comes then from man and not from God.

To do evil is to despise those eternal joys which

make the happiness of the soul, and which she can only lose in so far as she despises them and attaches herself to the false joys which are perishable and which can only be tasted by the mediation of the senses, that is to say by the lower nature of man (*De liber. Arbitr.*, I, xvi.) The cause of evil is not good, but the abandonment of good (*City of God*, xii. 9).

"I cannot sufficiently admire," says Bossuet when speaking of the error of the Manicheans as to the origin of evil, "that force of reasoning wherewith the incomparable St Augustine, and after him the great St Thomas his disciple, have refuted their extravagances.

"These great men taught them that they sought in vain for the efficient cause of evil; that evil being only a defect could not have a true cause, that all beings came from the first and sovereign Being who, as He is good in His own essence, so also communicates the impress of His goodness to all which comes forth from His hands; whence it manifestly results that there can be no creature evil by nature. . . .

"Thus, according to these great doctors, so far from the failures in creation proving that there are first causes and principles of evil, on the contrary it would be impossible that there should be any failure in the world if the first causes and principles were not good. For example there could be no irregularity if there were not a first, an invariable rule; nor could there be any malice in actions if there were not a sovereign goodness from which the wicked voluntarily turned aside" (Bossuet, *Deuxième sermon sur les démons*).

"Evil does not come from 'that which is,' but from 'that which is' being neither esteemed or loved as it ought to be. And if one asks how evil has entered into the reasonable creature in the midst of so many good things which God has put into him, one must simply remember that he is free and that he has been drawn from nothingness. Because he is free he can act; and because he is drawn from nothingness he can fail" (*De liber. Arbitr.*, xi.).

How could God be the author of evil since he has created not through necessity, but through loving kindness? Here again the germ of St Augustine's doctrine is found in the platonic philosophy. Indeed we read in the *Timaeus* of Plato: "Let us speak of the cause which made the supreme Ordainer produce and put together this universe. He was good, and he who is good has no sort of envy. Free from all envy he wished that everything should be as like himself as possible. He who follows the teaching of the wise and admits this as the principal reason for origin and formation of the world, will hold the truth."

Farther on when Plato represents God as starting with joy at the sight of His work; St Augustine recalls the words of Genesis on this subject: "And God saw that it was good." Then he adds: "In what sense must we understand these words repeated after each new creation: 'God saw that it was good' if not as an approbation given by God to His work as being made according to the rules of an art which is no other than His Wisdom. In truth God did not know that His work was good only after having made it, since He would not have made it if he had not known it good before He made it; therefore, when He says: 'It is good!' He does not learn, but he teaches.

"Plato went farther when he said that God started with joy when He finished the world. Assuredly Plato was too wise to believe that the novelty of creation could add to the Divine felicity; but he wished to make us understand that the work which pleased God before He made it pleased Him equally when he had made it.

"Thus, it is God who has made all things. And it is by his *Word* that he has made them since they are good. There is no more excellent workman than God, nor art more efficacious than His Word, nor is there any better reason for creation than this Word; a good work has been produced by a good workman. Plato whether he had read it in our books, or learnt it from those who had read it there, or whether the power of his genius raised him from the knowledge of the visible works of God to that of His invisible greatness, gives this same reason for the creation of the world and says that it was only reasonable for a good God to produce a good work" (*City of God*, xi. 21).

Creation is then the act of the Divine Almighty One who has drawn souls and bodies from nothingness,—a doctrine common to all "spiritualist" philosophers and to the Catholic Church: equally distant from Pantheism which identifies creation with the Creator, and Dualism which admits an uncreated matter, co-eternal with God. God could not find a substance from which to form his creatures independant of Himself, or incompatible with His infinite perfection, since He alone exists by Himself, and nothing can exist except by Him; and He has been able to draw from His own perfect and infinite substance, finite and imperfect creatures, since He alone is perfect.

He has created all from nothing, both spirit and matter, and were He to withdraw for a moment His creative power, all things would fall back into nothingness. He has created through pure loving-kindness, for the happiness of His creatures, inviting them to good, but giving to the superior creatures together with the dignity of free beings, the honour of embracing good by a voluntary choice, and the possibility of choosing evil by their own fault.

This weakness of human nature and its ready liability to these falls of which Augustine had had sad experience, no less than love of his neighbour, inspired him with indulgence for the guilty and made him wish for the softening of criminal legislation. He contended against the penalty of death which took away from the condemned the means of repentance and he protested against the "question by torture" which too often subjected the innocent to injustice.

"We in no way approve," he writes to Macedonius, an African bishop, "the faults which we wish may be corrected, and it is not because evil pleases us, that we demand indulgence for the evil-doer; but we pity the criminal while detesting the crime. The more we hate vice, the less are we willing that the vicious should perish before they have amended their life. It is common and natural to hate the wicked; but it is a rare and pious thing to love them because they are men, and in such a way that in the same person we can blame the fault and praise human nature, so that we shall with all the more justice hate evil because it has stained this nature that we love. To combat the crime and wish to deliver the criminal is not to engage oneself in the bonds of iniquity, but in the bonds of humanity. There is no other place but this world where one may correct oneself, for after this life we shall only have what we have here gathered together. It is therefore the love of men which makes us intercede for the guilty, fearful lest the punishment which ends their life should be a punishment without end. . . . Our intercession has sometimes consequences which we should not have wished. It may be that he whom we have saved grows bolder through this impunity, and that the hand of him whom we have snatched from death makes new victims: it may even happen that the sight of a guilty man pardoned and returning to a better life, may encourage and impel the bad to evil through the hope of going unpunished, but I do not believe that our intercession will be responsible for these ills. We have in view, and we wish only for what is good, the gentleness which makes the word of truth loved; we ask that those who are saved from a temporal death should live in such a way as not to fall into eternal death from which there is no deliverer. . . .

" What shall I say of the torture which they make an accused person submit to ? They want to know if he is guilty, and they begin by torturing him; for an uncertain crime, they impose, often on an innocent man, a certain penalty, not because they know the victim has committed the crime, but because they are in truth ignorant as to whether he has committed it; and what is still more odious and should appeal to our tears, is that the judge who orders the torture, for fear of killing an innocent man through ignorance, kills this same man by the very means he employs to save him from death.

"If, indeed, the victim prefers to give up life sooner than suffer the torture any longer, he will say that he is the author of the crime which he has not committed. Behold him then condemned, and put to death! And still the judge is ignorant if he has struck a guilty or an innocent man, the torture having proved useless to discover his innocence, and only having served to make him pass for guilty. Will a wise judge ascend the judgment-seat in the midst of such darkness? He certainly will, for society, whose cause he may not desert, proclaims it his duty. And he does not think it a crime to torture the innocent for the crimes of others, or to force them by the violence of torture to declare themselves falsely guilty, and to perish as such; or even if they escape condemnation, to be the cause of their dying from the consequences of the torture" (*Lett.* cxiii.).

Montesquieu's objection to this barbarous custom seems very timid beside that of St. Augustine, when, speaking of the torture, he limits himself to saying in Book VII. of *L'esprit des lois*: "We see it to-day rejected by a very civilized nation without bad results. It is not therefore essentially necessary."

Philosophy, whose proper object is the problem of human destiny, does not occupy itself with the destiny of the individual only, but still more with the destiny of mankind. This is what is called the philosophy of history. That of St. Augustine issues naturally from the Christian conception.

God created man, and all men come from one single man. Mankind grew from a single stem as if God had wished by giving them a common origin, to draw the bonds tighter which should unite them to each other. Thus men are akin to each other, not only by resemblance of nature, but by a real brotherhood (*City of God*, xii. 21).

According to Christian doctrine the unity of the human race is not that altogether exterior unity which a universal domination establishes by gathering all nations under its authority, and imposing on them the same language, the same laws, and the same customs. It is a spiritual unity which unites souls by the community of faith, charity, and hope, in a spiritual city, the Church of Jesus Christ, militant during time, and triumphant in eternity. As there is only one God who is the Father of all men, there is only one Church, and this Church gives all men the freedom of the city, on earth as well as in Heaven. This according to the Gospel is the beginning and end of humanity.

The Saviour came down to earth and died on the cross for all men; all are called to salvation. From His uplifted cross He has drawn to Himself the Jew and the idolater, the strong and the weak, the righteous and the sinner, all who are willing. " I when I am lifted up from the earth will draw all men unto me " (St John, xii. 32).

Distinctions of race, enmities of nations, inequalities of condition, all are effaced. " There is neither Jew nor Gentile, neither slave nor freeman, neither male nor female: but all are one in Jesus Christ," says St Paul (Gal., iii. 28). God raises up the human race from the abyss of the fall, enlightens little by little its darkened reason, strengthens its wavering will, and reëstablishes it by degrees in that peace which it lost through its sin.

This is the history of mankind according to the Gospel: in the Divine plan all culminates in the founding of that City which will establish the reign of God on earth as in Heaven: " Adveniat regnum tuum sicut in cœlo et in terra." This divine kingdom starting from the humblest beginnings, begun indeed by some fishermen of Galilee, will increase from age to age : " The kingdom of Heaven," says Christ, " is like unto a grain of mustard seed, which a man takes and sows in his field. It is the smallest of all seeds, but when it is grown up it is the greatest of all plants and it becomes a tree, and the birds of the air come and lodge in the branches thereof" (Matt. xiii. 31-2).

To arrive at this true land of promise, humanity traverses three great periods; first the time which preceded the law: " For until the law sin was in the world; but sin was not imputed, when the law was not " (Rom. v. 13). Then the time of the promise: "But before faith came, we were kept under the law shut up unto that faith which was to be revealed. Wherefore the law was our pedagogue in Christ, that we might be justified by faith" (Gal. iii. 23-4). Afterwards, the time of faith which came to fulfil the law: "So we also when we were children, were serving under the elements of the world. But when the fulness of the time was come God sent His Son, made of a woman, made under the law; That he might redeem them who were under the law; that we might receive the adoption of sons" (Gal. iv. 3, 4, 5).

It is in the third age that the divine promises were to be accomplished.

The inhabitants of earth and heaven were henceforth to form but one family, united by charity, a single body of which Jesus Christ should be the head. St Paul says, "That he might make known unto us the mystery of his will, according to his good pleasure, which he hath purposed in him, in the dispensation of the fulness of times, to reestablish all things in Christ that are in heaven and on earth in him" (Ephes. i. 9, 10).

Such is the final goal, indicated from all eternity, towards which Providence has led the human race since the creation of the world; the establishment of the City of the Saints in the House of God. "You are fellow-citizens with the saints and of the household of God, built upon the foundation of the apostles and prophets, Jesus Christ himself being the chief corner-stone, in whom all the building being framed together, groweth up into an holy temple in the Lord. In whom you also are built together into an habitation of God in the Spirit" (Ephes. ii. 19, 20, 21, 22).

It is this holy City which appeared to St John in the *Apocalypse* as the final consummation of all things: "He shewed me the holy city Jerusalem coming down out of heaven from God. And the city hath no need of the sun, nor of the moon, to shine upon it. For the glory of God hath enlightened it, and the Lamb is the lamp thereof" (*Apocal.* xxi. 10 and 23).

It is no longer the history of a privileged nation, of the Jewish people, drawn from debasement and freed from the servitude to which their enemies had reduced them, it is the history of all humanity, raised again from moral decadence, and enfranchised from the slavery of sin in the new Jerusalem. "It is this sense," says a learned commentator of apocalyptic literature, "that the Apocalypses are so many primitive essays on the philosophy of history" (*Réville, Litt. Apocalypt.*).

It is this new inspiration which guides Christian writers through history, and reveals to them *a law of progress*, which, under the impulse of Divine wisdom and goodness, governs the march and the development of humanity.

The ancient philosophers believed that this march of humanity was closely bound up with that of the universe, and as in their eyes the physical world containing an original principle of disorder, always moved in the circle of the returning *Great Year* with its periodical alternations of increase and decrease, so the human race was also condemned to these alternate periods of greatness and decline (*City of God*, xii. 14). With the Fathers of the Church, humanity, fallen in the beginning, is always raising itself by degrees, but being imperfect, it cannot rise to God without the help of His grace which leads it to walk willingly towards the goal appointed by His Providence. No one has set forth this philosophy of history better than St Augustine in his famous work *The City of God*. He begins in the first books by refuting the religious, philosophical and historical errors of heathendom. He re-writes eloquently the history of paganism which accused the Christians of the fall of the Roman Empire; he condemns its institutions, its doctrines, its customs; he vindicates Providence in the calamities which their own sins have drawn down on them; and then in sight of this afflicting spectacle he draws the consoling picture of the constant and undefined progress of the people of God, and shows that the first division of the sons of Adam into children of light and children of darkness, has gone on all through the centuries, and that the pagan philosophers were the sport of a chimera when they imagined some sort of circular and periodic revolution inevitably reproducing and bringing back the same beings in the same order into a universe always identical under its apparent transformations, perishing and being reborn in an eternal alternation. Here again St Augustine differs from Plato for whom the progress of the human race only consists in returning by a fatal law of alternation to its primitive state at the end of a determined period, just as by a sort of fatality of evil, and by the inherent decay of its imperfect nature, it insensibly deviated from its first condition (Plato, *Politic*).

The growth through the centuries of this common patrimony of light and justice, which bears the fair name of civilisation, was not conceived of for mankind by the Greeks or Romans. For them humanity like the universe moved in a circle where descent inevitably succeeded ascent. It started from the golden age, moving away from it progressively, then at a given moment it inevitably returned to recommence the same revolution in the periodic cycle in which the human generations move.

" Some philosophers," says St Augustine, " have invented I know not what revolutions of centuries, which incessantly reproduce and bring back the same beings, whether it be that they conceive these revolutions as being accomplished in the bosom of the same world which subsists under these successive transformations, or whether it be that the world perishes and is born again in an eternal alternation. Nothing is exempt from this vicissitude, not even the immortal soul ; for when it has reached wisdom, they make it pass from a false bliss to a misery which is only too true " (*City of God*, xii. 13).

Christianity on the contrary revealed to St Augustine faith in a better future according to the promise of Jesus Christ. In the first man, our common father, the struggle began which was to continue through the ages in all mankind, the struggle of good against evil, which becomes the struggle of the city of God inflamed by the Divine love, against the city of earth consumed by love of self. Here man is divided against himself, the house torn by dissensions, the city troubled by disorders and civil dissensions, the universe a prey to the violence of war, evil increasing and with it the City of Evil.

A nation destined to command the world, imposes its laws on the conquered nations by shedding oceans of human blood. "As God designed to use this empire to chastise a great number of nations, He entrusted it to men enamoured of praise and honour, who made their glory one with that of their native land, and were always ready to sacrifice themselves for her safety, thus triumphing over their covetousness and all their other vices by this single vice, the love of glory" (*City of God*, iv. 6; v. 13).

What misery in this apparent grandeur! But if we turn our eyes to the other side, we see that God in His infinite mercy wished to save fallen humanity, and promised it a deliverer by whom His Kingdom should be founded. He prefigured this heavenly kingdom, this divine city in a people whom He chose for Himself; and like those whose education is accomplished by degrees, He led them slowly through perils and obstacles which the children of earth raised up against them on all sides; He raised them little by little from the worship of temporal things to the worship of eternal things, from the visible to the invisible, until the day when He sent His Son on earth to reveal the whole truth to humanity, and to establish there for ever the reign of God (*City of God*, x. 14).

The life of the individual may be divided into six ages; the first infancy, during which he does not speak; childhood, when his intelligence awakes; boyhood; youth; maturity; old age. During the first ages, man lives almost altogether the life of the senses; in the following ages, the intellectual and moral life develops by degrees.

In the same way the people of God, the true representative of the human race traverses six ages: the first from Adam to Noah; the second from Noah to Abraham; the third from Abraham to David; the fourth from David to the captivity of Babylon; the fifth from the captivity of Babylon to the coming of Jesus Christ amongst men. The sixth is now being accomplished and will last until the end of the world. These six periods correspond with the six days of creation; and as the seventh day was the day of repose, the seventh age will be the age of eternal repose and of beatitude, when the interior man who is renewed from day to day shall have attained his perfection.

Such is the law of progress which governs the history of humanity, and of which even those who fight against it become instruments in the hands of Providence according to the Divine plan (*City of God*, x. 14).

The history of the human race and its development through the ages is at the same time the progress of the city of God which grows from century to century, and the decay of the terrestrial city which is ever declining and tending towards its ruin.

"On one side we see this earthly city clouded by error, dominated by lusts, divided against itself in struggles where the weak are the prey of the strong. God who rules the destiny of empires permits the empires of the East to succeed the Roman empire, so as to lead men to political unity; then in its turn this empire must crumble to make way for the Kingdom of God, and the unity of men in God."

"On the other side we follow the progress of the elect people, from Adam to Jesus Christ; that is to say the progress of humanity in true faith which extends from day to day, and little by little will conquer the universe."

Two loves have built two cities. The love of self carried to scorn of God, has built the city of earth; the love of God carried to scorn of self, that of Heaven; one glorifies itself in itself, the other glorifies itself in the Lord; one aspiring to human glory is inflated with pride, the other says to God : 'Thou art all my glory;' one is intoxicated with its own power, the other says to God: 'Thou art my strength.' In one, princes oppress their subjects, in the other, princes are united with their subjects. In one reigns gross superstition, or the false science of the sages of the world, who, if they have known God, have never rendered Him the homage which is His due, and are lost in the vanity of their own thoughts; in the other reigns true wisdom, together with that faith which founds the worship of the true God, and which in the society of the saints (that is to say in the society of holy men and angels), awaits its reward in the accomplishment of this word: "God all in all" (*City of God*, xv., *passim*).

"Thus the destinies of mankind, like the course of nature, depend on Him who exists immutable above all things which pass away, He who alone possesses supreme wisdom with sovereign power, who has assigned to all creatures the beginning and end of their existence, who governs all causes and disposes of them according to His eternal counsels. He knows all events private or public before they are accomplished, He directs them by His power and His wisdom, and still He allows the beings whom He has created free to act freely. Man is not able by his sin to disturb the eternal designs of God, and oblige Him to alter His purposes, since God has foreseen how far man whom He created good would become bad, and what good He Himself could draw from man's malice" (*City of God*, xiv. 11).

God, while leaving men full liberty and the entire responsibility of their actions, both in their resolutions and their efforts to accomplish them, reserves to Himself the power of making the success or failure of their resolutions and the consequences of their efforts, which do not like resolution and effort depend on their free will, turn to His sovereign ends. The will of individuals, and that of nations, of those who direct, as of those who are directed, remains independent; it is the will which does what they wish to do, but the consequences are in the hands of God. Thus the two principles, human liberty and Divine omniscience which the true philosopher confesses as well as the true Christian, are reconciled without effort (*City of God*, v. 10).

Sinners can do nothing to derange the economy of the great works of God in which His will is always accomplished, as He dispenses to every creature what should belong to him, with a wisdom equal to His power, He knows how to use not only the good but also the wicked (*City of God*, xiv. 27).

This philosophy of history was afterwards to be Bossuet's in the *Discours sur l'histoire universelle*. He explains, like St Augustine, how the free will of men is reconciled in history with the providential plan. "They do more, or less, as they can," says Bossuet, "and their councils have never failed to bring about unforeseen consequences. . . . There is no human power which does not serve in spite of itself other designs than its own; God alone knows how to subdue all to His will" (*Hist. univ.*, iii. 7).

Thus man remains master of his will, but the consequences of his voluntary act pass beyond him; a superior will disposes of them—Providence, who leads humanity to its goal. And as God does not bind our free-will because He foresees by His prescience what our free resolutions will be, so neither does He fetter it by His Providence because He draws results which we had not foreseen from our free resolutions, and makes them serve His eternal counsels.

APPENDIX

Page 14. The fact that St Augustine has left us a list of retractations ought to impress upon us the truth that the opinion of no single Father is to be regarded as infallible, and that even the consent of all together has no inherent force except so far as it witnesses to the teaching of the Church in matters of faith and morals. We are certainly free to think that his doctrine touching the character of infants in this world, and their fate (if unbaptised) in the next, is severe and out of harmony with the mind of the Church as since unfolded to us by the process of doctrinal evolution. Still, there are some considerations which should temper our judgment in the matter. One is the stress laid by St Augustine on what is called 'material sin,' the inculpable transgression of God's law. It is our tendency and error to regard such transgression as of no consequence, as involving no matter for regret, or restitution, or prevention; and to reserve the term 'sin' for culpable breaches of law. We should not consider, *e.g.*, the livid jealousy of this babe, whom he here describes, very pretty; yet we excuse it from all sinfulness because it is not a free act. But Augustine looks to the moral ugliness of the act apart from all personal imputability. He sees in it a tendency which, when reason wakes, we are ashamed of, and strive to overcome and to root out as unfitting our spiritual dignity. It is one of those many manifestations of the tyranny of our lower self, which, though 'natural' in one sense, is nevertheless a fruit of original sin as understood by St Augustine. As to the fate of unbaptised infants hereafter, in making the pain of loss in some sense positive he and others differ from many who regard it as purely negative. There is the loss of one who is born blind and is never told it; and of one who has enjoyed sight and lost it; and between the two there is the loss of one who is born blind and knows he has lost he knows not what, and is pained by the thought. Such is the pain St Augustine seems to anticipate for unbaptised infants. His description or colouring of the pain is no part of the substance of his doctrine. Lastly, his treatment of the orchard escapade of his boyhood seems at first sight to be much ado about nothing. But in truth, as he elsewhere insists so explicitly, the violation of conscience is the soul of every sin, whether it be in the little things of childhood or in the greater concerns of manhood. Nay, may it not be said that the first sins, by which conscience's fine edge is blunted for ever, are in some sense the worst? Was not the resistance to grace more wilful and the remorse more bitter? There is something *sui generis* and decisive about a child's first lie or first theft that has no measure in the triviality of the matter. Besides, in his acute analysis of this theft, what St Augustine deplores is that it was committed not thoughtlessly, nor yet through greediness, as is so often the case with children's pilferings, but for sheer love of wrong-doing: "I flung them away, enjoying nothing thereof but the iniquity, in which I was delighted. For if any of that fruit entered my mouth nothing made it agreeable to me but sin." In a word, it was a sin not of frailty but of malice.

Page 44. 'Probabilism' is more commonly used now-a-days to denote an ethical theory in reference to the formation of our conscience in cases of uncertainty. Here, it is appropriated to the theory of the Academics who denied the possibility of speculative certainty of any kind, though allowing a sufficient approximation to the truth for all practical purposes of life.

Page 72. This does not imply that according to Catholic teaching the faculty of choice, or any other natural faculty of the soul, has been intrinsically warped or injured by original sin; but only that the soul has been penally dispossessed of certain gratuitous supernatural gifts by which alone it could attain to a supernatural heaven or salvation, altogether above what would have otherwise been its natural heaven or salvation. Also, that the soul is by Adam's sin deprived of many external helps and favourable circumstances and conditions by which its salvation would have been facilitated. We may not dare to say dogmatically that God could not, consistently with His goodness and mercy, have created and intended such a world of ignorance, infirmity and sin as we see around us; but we may say that had He done so it would

APPENDIX 153

have been a mystery to reason, implying some hidden explanation such as revelation actually gives us in the story of the Fall.

Page 86. The physiological necessity of death is a thought foreign to all primitive people. They regard death as externally inevitable, just as slips and mistakes are inevitable in the gross, though singly avoidable; but that age and decline is a continuation of the same process which is called growth in its earlier stage is a conclusion of more scientific times. Death is indeed natural to man considered physiologically; but, historically speaking, he was endowed at his creation with a preternatural immortality, subsequently forfeited by the sin whose punishment reduced him to his natural poverty in this and other respects.

Page 87. St Augustine prescinds everywhere from the hypothetical 'state of mere nature,' and speaks of man historically, not scientifically. Whence Lutherans have taken occasion for their doctrine of an intrinsic perversion of man's natural faculties, spiritual and bodily, consequent on the fall; as though immortality, perfect enlightenment, perfect self-control, as well as a destiny to the facial vision of God were essentials of our being, only forfeited through sin. The Church holds these prerogatives to be altogether preternatural and supernatural; the 'innocence' of original justice is not negative, not mere sinlessness; but the possession of a positive spiritual grace altogether supernatural. 'Original sin' is merely the absence of that gift in one to whom it was historically, though not naturally, due; and who has forfeited it by an ancestral, not by any personal fault. The doctrine of original sin, like that of the atonement, rests on the conception of humanity as a corporation or organism of which each member shares the destiny of the whole for better or for worse, and none can afford to say: 'Am I my brother's keeper?' At root it is the doctrine of Christian charity, the one antidote for the follies of both socialism and individualism.

Page 92. Plainly there is no 'Jansenism' in this text nor in the idea drawn from it. It was in forgetting that St Augustine in his controversy with the Pelagians necessarily concentrated his mind on one side of the truth, and in taking him as the *ex professo* exponent of the other, which he had left to look after itself for the time being, that the Jansenists deviated from orthodoxy; still more, no doubt, in a certain spirit of puritanical severity which made semi-Calvinistic views very congenial to them. Combating the usurpations of liberty Augustine had no need to assert and defend its rights; claiming for grace its bare due he was not concerned to guard against an excessive claim. But where he was only intent on denial the Jansenists build on his implicit affirmation, and conversely.

In respect to human liberty he shows more than once his clear recognition of that problem which is coeval with the human race; on the one hand the ineradicable conviction of our responsibility, on the other, the inconceivableness of self-determination, without which responsibility seems unthinkable,—not to speak of the difficulty suggested as to the completeness of the Divine foreknowledge. Here it seems we have an eternal antinomy of the human reason, the truth hiding safe between two opposite statements, each of which glances on one side or other of the mark, though both together encompass it. Wisely does the Catholic Church allow and encourage the pacific coexistence of both statements in her schools, that by their wholesome hostility they may keep one another in check, lest the prevalence of one side of the truth should ever cause the other to be forgotten or obscured.

Page 110. St Augustine's opposition to the rather reasonable view of St Jerome in this point was dictated by the singularly strict definition of a lie which he adopted, and by which, apart from all consideration of the evil motives or ill consequences to oneself or others, apart from the cowardice, meanness, injury, injustice, social insecurity, and all the reasons usually insisted on by moralists, he found a certain absolute and intrinsic malice in a lie simply regarded as an abuse of speech. Herein he is followed by Aquinas, and by many, if not most, Western theologians; though not, I think, by any of the Protestant divines, who in this matter hold rather with the wider views of the Eastern Fathers. These latter allow a lie (called perhaps by some other name) when the aforesaid objectionable causes and consequences are absent or justifiable. St Augustine's doctrine gave birth later to the doctrine of equivocation, whereby similar emergencies were provided for, by an endeavour to reconcile a literal adhesion to the truth with the liberty of self-defence which the opposite

APPENDIX

school sought more boldly, though perhaps less philosophically. The problem still awaits solution.

Page 118. The Cartesian argument is no doubt a refutation of *absolute* scepticism, but it leaves a relative or modified scepticism intact, except so far as further consequences equally undeniable can be deduced from that one first principle. Nay, it encourages practical scepticism by implying that doubt is reasonable in every case where equally irresistible evidence is not forthcoming. Here St Augustine would have protested.

Page 121. In consequence of this view of the relation between soul and body, an opinion obtained among some mediæval theologians that a state of permanent disembodiment would be opposed to the natural exigencies of the human soul; and therefore that, apart from the glorified resurrection won for us by Christ, man in the merely natural order would have had a title to some kind of resurrection or re-embodiment; just as in so many other respects he seems to be of all creatures the most helpless in regard to his highest needs, the most dependent on divine intervention and succour. Such a view would more easily gain ground where the physiological necessity of death was not clearly recognised; still more where there was any tendency to the Lutheran confusion of the preternatural with the natural prerogatives of our first parents. Though tenable, the view is not common now, nor has it any but speculative and historical interest.

G. T.

The Saints.

The Series is under the General Editorship of M. HENRI JOLY, formerly Professor at the Sorbonne and at the Collège de France, author of numerous works upon Psychology; and the authorised English translations are having, and will continue to have, the advantage of the revision of the Rev. Father TYRRELL, S.J., who contributes to each volume a Preface and, in some cases, a few Notes addressed especially to English readers.

In order to give a true idea of the nature of the volumes, the publishers give below some passages from the letter addressed by the General Editor of the Series to his collaborators.

"In a very remarkable letter upon the true method of writing the lives of the Saints, Mgr. Dupanloup did not hesitate to say that, 'there are very few lives of the Saints written as they should be,' and he asks for this work, 'Above and beyond everything else a love of the Saint, then a profound study of his life and spirit from original sources and contemporary documents, then the portraiture of this soul and its struggles, and of what nature and grace were in it; all this traced with simplicity, truthfulness, dignity, deep penetration and impressive detail, in such a way that the Saint and his times may be faithfully represented, but nevertheless so that the presentation of the contemporary facts of history may not blur the picture of the Saint, who should always remain the most prominent figure in his story; true and authentic facts, briefly set forth, but arranged with skill and cleverly disposed, in a scholarly sequence preparing for and illuminating every-

THE SAINTS

thing;'—the precaution of 'making the Saint himself tell his own story, without which everything living and individual is apt to disappear, and thus all Saints are made to resemble one another; . . . a style, in short, simple, reverent, touching and penetrative.'

"That all these qualities have been often enough united in works worthy of being studied we are very far from denying . . . but it has been in the case of quarto books or in works in more than one volume. It has therefore been thought opportune to present a living portrait of each of the great Saints in a more restrained form, in order to draw attention to it and perhaps to re-form the ideas of a much larger circle of readers."

The following passage, taken from an article by the English Editor in *The Month* for December 1897, entitled "What is Mysticism?" will also be of use as a further indication of the spirit in which the books are being written:—

"The old time-honoured Saint's Life, with its emphasis on the miraculous and startling features of the portrait, its suppression of what was natural, ordinary, and therefore presumably uninteresting, and consequently its abandonment of all attempt to weave the human and divine into one truthful and harmonious whole, showing the gradual evolution of the perfect from the imperfect, to many minds makes no appeal whatever. . . . All this points to the need of what we might call a more subjective treatment of Saints' lives than we have been accustomed to; and it is to this that the 'Psychologie des Saints' addresses itself. We need less than formerly to be dazzled with the wonderful, and more to be drawn to the lovable. We want to be put *en rapport* with the Saints, to feel their humanity, to interpret it by our own, and thereby to realise that no miracle they ever wrought is comparable to the miracle of what they were."

THE SAINTS

The first volumes will be as follows:—

THE PSYCHOLOGY OF THE SAINTS.

By HENRI JOLY, formerly Professor at the Sorbonne and at the Collège de France. Author of "L'homme et l'animal"; "Psychologie des grands hommes," &c.

S. AUGUSTINE.

By AD. HATZFELD, joint-collaborator with Arsène Darmesteter in the "Dictionnaire Général de la Langue Française."

S. CLOTILDA.

By GODEFROY KURTH, Professor at the University of Liège. Author of "Histoire poétique des Mérovingiens," "Clovis," &c.

S. VINCENT DE PAUL.

By PRINCE EMMANUEL DE BROGLIE, Lauréat de l'Académie française.

Further volumes will be announced in due course.

LONDON: DUCKWORTH & CO.

www.ingramcontent.com/pod-product-compliance
Lightning Source LLC
Chambersburg PA
CBHW022116160426
43197CB00009B/1045